20
50

DESIGNING OUR
TOMORROW

ARCHITECTURAL DESIGN
July/August 2015

Profile
No 236

Guest-Edited by
CHRIS LUEBKEMAN

Concept art for *Minority Report*, 20th Century Fox, 2002

26

ISSN 0003-8504
ISBN 978-1118-914830

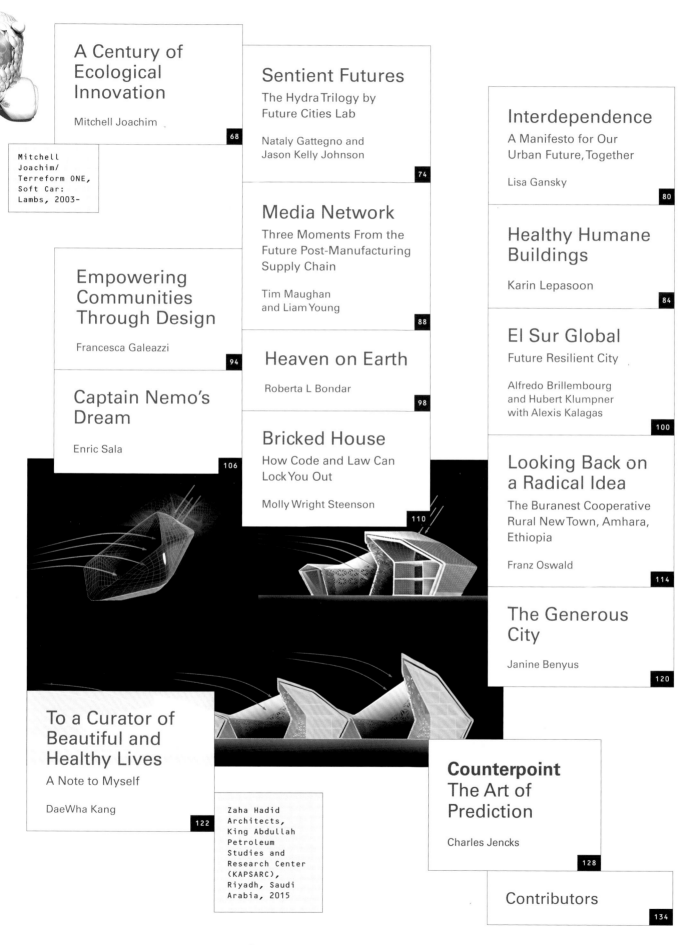

Editorial Offices
John Wiley & Sons
25 John Street
London WC1N 2BS
UK

T +44 (0)20 8326 3800

Editor
Helen Castle

Managing Editor (Freelance)
Caroline Ellerby

Production Editor
Elizabeth Gongde

Prepress
Artmedia, London

Art Direction + Design
CHK Design:
Christian Küsters
Sophie Troppmair

Printed in Italy by Printer
Trento Srl

Front cover: Zio Ziegler, *In the age of simulacra and simulation*, February 2015. © Zio Ziegler, with adaptations to the original by Mark Pearsall

Inside front cover: SHoP, Cladding pattern study: perforated and solid acrylic, 3D print. © SHoP Architects, photo Jenna Clingenpeel

04/2015

MIX
Paper from responsible sources
FSC
www.fsc.org   FSC® C015829

ARCHITECTURAL DESIGN

July/August	Profile No.
2015	236

Journal Customer Services
For ordering information, claims and any enquiry concerning your journal subscription please go to www.wileycustomerhelp .com/ask or contact your nearest office.

Americas
E: cs-journals@wiley.com
T: +1 781 388 8598 or
+1 800 835 6770 (toll free in the USA & Canada)

Europe, Middle East and Africa
E: cs-journals@wiley.com
T: +44 (0) 1865 778315

Asia Pacific
E: cs-journals@wiley.com
T: +65 6511 8000

Japan (for Japanese-speaking support)
E: cs-japan@wiley.com
T: +65 6511 8010 or 005 316 50 480 (toll-free)

Visit our Online Customer Help available in 7 languages at www.wileycustomerhelp .com/ask

Print ISSN: 0003-8504
Online ISSN: 1554-2769

Prices are for six issues and include postage and handling charges. Individual-rate subscriptions must be paid by personal cheque or credit card. Individual-rate subscriptions may not be resold or used as library copies.

All prices are subject to change without notice.

Identification Statement
Periodicals Postage paid at Rahway, NJ 07065. Air freight and mailing in the USA by Mercury Media Processing, 1850 Elizabeth Avenue, Suite C, Rahway, NJ 07065, USA.

USA Postmaster
Please send address changes to *Architectural Design,* c/o Mercury Media Processing, 1634 E. Elizabeth Avenue, Linden, NJ 07036, USA.

Subscribe to D
D is published bimonthly and is available to purchase on both a subscription basis and as individual volumes at the following prices.

Prices
Individual copies:
£24.99 / US$39.95
Individual issues on
D App for iPad:
£9.99 / US$13.99
Mailing fees for print may apply

Annual Subscription Rates
Student: £75 / US$117
print only
Personal: £120 / US$189
print and iPad access
Institutional: £212 / US$398
print or online
Institutional: £244 / US$457
combined print and online
6-issue subscription on
D App for iPad: £44.99 /
US$64.99

New millennia are apocalyptic; turns of the century are epochal. Mid centuries, however, provide a quintessential focal point or Lydian stone. When in January 2000, for instance, ᴐ marked the turn of the new millennium with the *Millennium Architecture* issue, Charles Jencks drove the debate, in the shadow of the millennium bug and prophesies of Armageddon, by questioning the underlying worldview 2,000 years after Christ's birth, asking whether society was now fundamentally sacred or secular. The architecture of millennium projects, fuelled by the funding of the National Lottery in the UK, epitomised by the empty space and the vacuous curation of the Millennium Dome, were featured cheek by jowl with the newly built churches of Rome. In this issue, 2050 becomes a significant mark in the sand for future speculation. Guest-Editor Chris Luebkeman, engineer, architect, thought leader, upbeat visionary and Director for Global Foresight + Research + Innovation at Arup, puts his foot on the accelerator and pushes the fast-forward button. He asks us to project our minds 35 years forth and boldly imagine what might be the complex state and challenges in the hyper-urbanised, intensely populated world of tomorrow.

From our earliest conversations around this issue, Chris was adamant about the spirit in which it was to be realised. Despite the seemingly catastrophic future in which we are being propelled, which will most certainly be characterised by climate change, an increasing number of natural disasters, scarcity of resources, unprecedented population growth and greater inequality among people around the world, he insisted on an optimistic and constructive approach. In the introduction, he asks architects to face up to the seemingly cataclysmic realities that the next few decades hold, to apply their skills as problem-solvers, and 'to design places and spaces that not only empower people to survive in this world, but to thrive'. This is borne out by his invitation to influential design thinkers such as MoMA curator Paola Antonelli, eminent production designer Alex McDowell and CEO and President of IDEO Tim Brown, to commentate on the power of design to imagine and bring about effective change.

The vision of 2050 that emerges embraces today's reality: it is one that lacks the smooth slickness of previously utopian, modernist models. It captures a multiplicity of voices from a wide range of disciplines and regions. Within its pages it takes us from San Francisco to rural communities in China and Ethiopia, and the urban chaos of Brazil's favelas. It is as local as it is global. Key touching-points remain: an emphasis on the highly connected future that new technologies have ushered in, and a concern with sustainability and wellbeing. Architecture is rethought afresh, as architects become by turn implementers of robotic-designed constructions, hands-on self-builders and curators of environments that engineer wellbeing and beauty. What is apparent is that nothing can stand still and the resolve to tackle the challenges thrown at us by climate change, environmental damage and dwindling natural resources loom large on the horizon as pressing and unavoidable imperatives. ᴐ

Drivers of
Change cards

Chris Luebkeman led his team at Arup
to produce and publish the Drivers of
Change cards as a tool to help people and
organisations have thoughtful conversations
about the factors shaping our society.
Each card presents a different issue, asks a
provocative question, and uses succinct text
and colourful infographics to spark robust
debate among readers.

Chris Luebkeman

Innovation Workshop

TED Global

Edinburgh

2013

As a futurist and skilled facilitator, leading
workshops is a powerful means for Chris to
fulfil his mission of advocating for innovation.
The TED community, which Chris has been
deeply involved with for over a decade, often
calls upon him to lead discussions aimed
at reifying their most exciting ideas. At a
workshop hosted by the Kauffman Foundation
in 2013, Chris helps explore how the TED
community can support entrepreneurship

Danish Maritime Forum
Closing Plenary

Copenhagen

October

2014

Chris fosters a culture of intellectual
curiosity and creativity within his team at
Arup and in all his outward-facing activities.
Here he was invited by the Value Web to
moderate a three-day event, which brought
together international maritime industry
leaders – José María Figueres (President
of the Carbon War Room), Esben Poulsson
(Chairman of AVRA International), Andreas
Sohmen-Pao (CEO of BW Group) and Henrik
O Madsen (Group President and CEO of DNV
GL) – under the patronage of the Danish
Royal Family and Government.

Chris Luebkeman has been described by *The Guardian* newspaper as the 'Willy Wonka of the built environment, conjuring up dreams of a future where we can cure our ills through faith, physics and forethought'.[1] An unabashed and unapologetic optimist, he helps people and organisations pause to think about the world we are all co-creating. *Wallpaper** magazine cited him as one of the 10 future speculators and shapers 'who will change the way we live'.[2]

Luebkeman spends half of his time travelling the world observing the faces and facets of change. He is an active participant in conferences ranging in scope from those of the Design Futures Council to TED and the World Economic Forum, is a popular keynote speaker on topics relating to the future, an agile facilitator of difficult conversations and an interactive panel member. He is fascinated by the world we live in and its infinite definitions of 'normal'.

His curiosity is reflected in his varied formal education: geology and civil engineering at Vanderbilt University in Tennessee, structural engineering at Cornell and a doctorate from the School of Architecture at the ETH Zurich.

An Arup Fellow and the company's Director for Global Foresight + Research + Innovation (a group he helped create), Luebkeman proudly leads a global team that facilitates conversations about how to best embrace change and its effects on the built environment. In *Drivers of Change* (Prestel, 2009), with the Foresight team he looked at the most important factors that would/will affect our world, arranged in a framework known as STEEP (social, technological, economic, environmental and political). Designed as a collection of notecards, the book provided a tool for developing business strategy, brainstorming and education, or simply to think creatively and holistically. The aim was to encourage deeper consideration of the forces driving global change and the role that individuals can play in creating a more sustainable future.

Luebkeman believes the future is a story that each of us participates in writing every day. He encourages us all to dig in because it is only when tomorrow transitions to yesterday that we will have the clarity of hindsight to know what the future really was. ⌂

This issue would not have been possible without the patience, diligence, perseverance and unwavering support of Radha Mistry. Thank you.

Notes
1. Stephen Armstrong, 'The Futurist', *Guardian Magazine*, 24 September 2005, p 1: www.theguardian.com/science/2005/sep/24/comment.comment.
2. Claire Dowdy, 'ALL CHANGE: Ten Who Will Change the Way We Live', *Wallpaper**, July/August 2002, p 31.

20

Can You

David Taylor

Built Up

Goat Canyon

US-Mexico border

Tijuana-San Ysidro

2009

Walls are built for many reasons. They can be virtual or physical. The canyon was a conduit for thousands who were searching desperately for a better tomorrow. It was terraformed by the Army Corps of Engineers to allow for easier border surveillance and enforcement. Rather than identifying ourselves as simply belonging to a nation, separated by physical borders, we must embrace the idea of global citizenship.

Imagine ...?

The future is fiction. It is the story each one of us is actively writing every day of our lives. The storyline is bound by that which we are all humbly aware waits for no one and nothing: time. It is the singular constant that, at least at this point, cannot be manipulated. Everything else is 'on the table'. To consider what our world will be like 35 years hence is an exercise of conjecture. Yet, just as a beams of light can illuminate our way ahead, consideration of global trends can help us discern where paths converge and point us towards some constructive conclusions.

Our world is a complex place. It is a chaotic cacophony of interacting and intersecting systems. In order to determine some intrinsic order of these systems we need to view them through five distinct lenses: social, technological, environmental, economic and political (otherwise known as STEEP). The challenges of the hyper-urbanised world of 2050 will have an ever-increasing velocity, veracity and complexity. The frameworks and solutions that have worked so well for us for the past 200 years will no longer be sufficient to serve us. And, just as a good therapist will ask a patient to face his or her issues head on, we need to look the complexity before us squarely in the eye and name it, so that we can set about the work of dealing with it.

Elizabeth Gill Lui

Stop and Hear the Music

Dorsoduro

Venice

2014

We are part of everything happening, as well as part of what the future holds, even if we are contemplative and static amid the dynamic chaos around us. As the English poet and Church of England cleric John Donne (1572–1631) said: 'No man is an island.'

Steve McCurry

Man at the Red Cross hospital reads to a boy

Kandahar

Afghanistan

1985

A photo full of rich stories. The trans-generational exchange, the beauty of two humans connecting, the joy on their faces and the terrible physical loss of each. Our will – our indomitable spirit – will carry us into whatever the future holds.

No man is an island.

— John Donne (1572–1631)

Facing the Facts

It is time to get brutally honest about where we stand. Yet, no one enjoys bad news. We naturally want to ignore the challenges of overpopulation and species degradation, of our oceans turning acidic, and the true price to our global civilisation of the Grand Canyon-sized wealth gap. These challenges, which are very real today, can be overwhelming and are easy to ignore for those not used to dealing with complexity.

But behold the architect. The very practice of architecture demands a synthesis of right- and left-brain thinking. Architects are the ultimate problem solvers, trained specifically to deal with and negotiate complexity through design. Daily they juggle into balance human emotions, physical constraints, environmental assaults, climate impacts, political frameworks and beleaguered budgets. This uniquely positions them to truly tackle so many of the problems facing the planet.

To help do my part as a futurist, I believe there is great benefit in looking at our systems separately, through the STEEP lenses, so that we can appreciate their interaction in our own minds and practice. At the end of the day, our goal is to design places and spaces that not only empower people to survive in this world, but to thrive. As we do this, we cannot gate ourselves from the things we do not like. This 1950s attitude simply will no longer cut it.

Steve McCurry

Women bathing at the Teej Festival

Kathmandu

Nepal

1984

In the end it is love we should always focus on. It is a wondrous, joyous amalgam that binds us all together on this slowly turning planet we call home.

Our goal is to design places and spaces that not only empower people to survive in this world, but to thrive

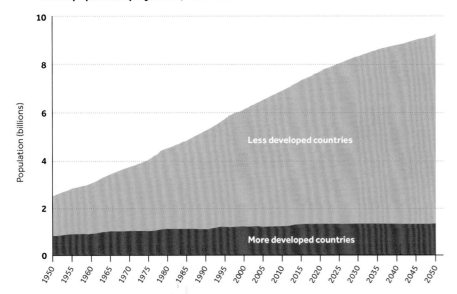

Global population projection, 1950–2050

Population (billions)

Less developed countries

More developed countries

Nothing about the future of humanity on the planet is guaranteed. If we continue to proliferate as expected, then the United Nations Population Division published this graph as the projection for the population.

Source

United Nations Department of Economic and Social Affairs Population Division, *World Population Prospects: The 2008 Revision*, United Nations (New York), 2009: www.un.org/esa/population/publications/wpp2008/wpp2008_highlights.pdf

Global Citizenship

Indeed, we need to broaden our definition of 'citizenship'. As a child in grade school, along with every other American child in public schools in the early 1960s, I recited, hand over heart and en masse, the Pledge of Allegiance at the beginning of every day. It was a narrow view – my citizenship clearly ended at my national boundary. Now we must extend this pledge to make citizenship a global idea. It needs to be understood as a responsibility to the ever-increasing number of our fellow world citizens, and even further, an obligation to the planet itself.

True, cancer and viruses like Ebola are fighting back, but if we assume that nature does not overcome the current pace of human behaviour, we will have a planet in 2050 with a significantly increased population. How significant? When I was born in 1961, I had about three billion neighbours. We are on track to hit nine billion by 2050. For a planet that has not grown a smidge in size, a tripling in just shy of 100 years brings into sharp focus the earth's carrying capacity or the maximum population it can sustain. Will there be a meaningful existence for all those nine billion beings? I hope so.

The world's population will be older in 2050, a by-product of advances in medicine and changing birth rates. Certain countries are getting younger,[1] with women bringing up to eight babies into the world, whereas many others are getting older[2] with a birth rate too low to sustain the current population. A peek behind the scenes of any business will tell you that a society needs young people to do work. Eighty-year-olds do not make for vibrant stock clerks or construction labourers. Where there are young people, so goes the work and money quickly follows. Thanks to Deng Xiaoping's One Child policy introduced in 1978, China has many more elderly today than ever before as a proportion of its total population. Population pyramids give us a very clear picture of the shape of a society, a nation, a region or a city. They help us understand the context of the infrastructure a society needs while telling us of future human migration patterns. Do you know if your city, region or nation is getting younger or older? Have you thought about the impact on your neighbourhood of the changing shape of the pyramid?

Inclusion

All young people are not treated equally today. As we look forward to 2050, global citizenry must help girls get into, and stay, in school longer. This is the keystone to all other issues. When women are empowered, many other systems (the economy, politics, social structure, even the environment) are impacted in a positive way, and for generations. Educated girls start micro-businesses and learn to manage money. They put food on the table, make sure children are in school and create more stable communities. They are, and will be, the backbone of a strong global community.

With both male and female members of society equally educated in every part of the world, our environment stands to benefit. It will need it. Our lifestyle is killing the other inhabitants of our planet at an alarming rate. We have lost 76 per cent of the freshwater species since 1970.[3] Our lifestyle is also killing us. Air pollution from stoves, cars, fires and factories and small engines is a prime culprit. We can absolutely do something about air quality starting today in the same way that we did something about fluorocarbons in the 1970s.

Global population pyramid, 1950–2050

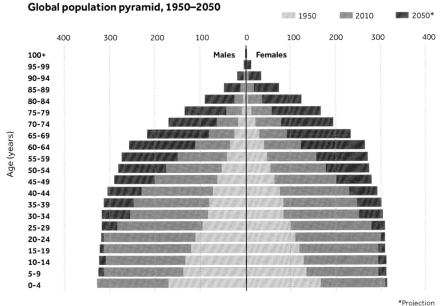

Legend: 1950 | 2010 | 2050*

Males | Females

Age (years): 100+, 95-99, 90-94, 85-89, 80-84, 75-79, 70-74, 65-69, 60-64, 55-59, 50-54, 45-49, 40-44, 35-39, 30-34, 25-29, 20-24, 15-19, 10-14, 5-9, 0-4

X-axis: 400, 300, 200, 100, 0, 100, 200, 300, 400

*Projection

The men are on the left and the women on the right; age bands are vertically oriented. The longer the bar, the more people in the band.

Source

The Economist OnLine, 'The World in 2100', 13 May 2011, after data from the United Nations: http://www.economist.com/blogs/dailychart/2011/05/world_population

Ocean acidification, 1850–2100

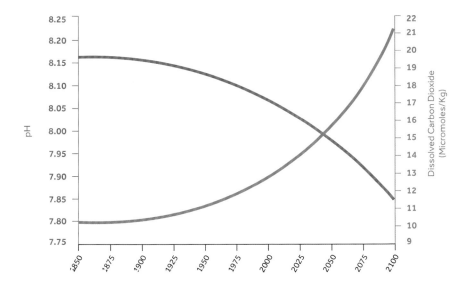

Left axis: pH — 8.25, 8.20, 8.15, 8.10, 8.05, 8.00, 7.95, 7.90, 7.85, 7.80, 7.75

Right axis: Dissolved Carbon Dioxide (Micromoles/Kg) — 22, 21, 20, 19, 18, 17, 16, 15, 14, 13, 12, 11, 10, 9

X-axis: 1850, 1875, 1900, 1925, 1950, 1975, 2000, 2025, 2050, 2075, 2100

The pH of the ocean is steadily decreasing, which is acidification.

Source

Richard A Feely, Christopher L Sabine and Victoria J Fabry, 'Carbon Dioxide and Our Ocean Legacy', Pacific Marine Environmental Laboratory Science Briefing, National Oceanic and Atmospheric Administration (NOAA), April 2006: www.pmel.noaa.gov/pubs/PDF/feel2899/feel2899.pdf

Delusion

The earth's lungs are at risk. Our oceans and forests create an atmosphere that we can breathe, and both are under great stress. This is a big deal because in addition to creating oxygen, our oceans supply the vast majority of the world's protein. Already today, phytoplankton – those microscopic organisms that make up the foundation of the aquatic food chain and feed everything from 150-tonne whales to invisible zooplankton – are dying off because of the increasing acidification of our oceans. Besides acting as food, they consume carbon dioxide and release oxygen. Oceanographers are terrified of the implications. Once the world cannot get its protein from fish, where will we dine?

Like a toddler playing with a supercomputer keyboard, we are messing with systems that are fundamentally unknown to us. We already see new weather patterns and extreme events, and we know the sea level is rising. By 2050, the most promising estimates say it will rise 30 centimetres more (almost a foot); more dire predictions say closer to 60 (close to 2 feet). Very few of the world's cities that line our oceans will be able handle this new normal. The future decisions we will be making on this issue alone will make our contemporary challenges look like child's play.

If Technology is the Answer, What is the Question?

All is not lost however. I am hopeful that technological innovation can solve some of these challenges. I agree with computer scientist Alan Kay, who defines technology as 'anything that was invented after you were born'.[4] Who today would consider the home refrigerator as technology? Other things that we have forgotten about will be rediscovered over the next 35 years. For example, if the pencil were invented today, it would be heralded as one of the most mind-blowing gadgets ever created. A device that can write anywhere and does not require energy to function – how incredible is that? Architects once used ink to draw on vellum, then on Mylar, with each stroke an intentional and considered permanent mark. This gave way to the ever-increasing temporality of lines on a 'desktop' the size of which would not have even served the simplest of tasks 35 years ago. When we slingshot forward 35 years, it will be all tools and techniques that were considered science fiction a few years ago that will be commonplace and taken for granted; a *Star Trek* holo-deck creative design space will be on the drawing boards and climate-adjusted real-time scenario-based modelling mandatory.

The future decisions we will be making on this issue alone will make our contemporary challenges look like child's play.

Chris Luebkeman

Ascending	The future is fiction. It is the story we write every day. As we move ever towards writing our story of tomorrow, we must hold dearly to the belief it will be a better place.
London	
2015	

出口 ⑦ EXIT →
四条通り（北）方面

Technological advances in computation, medicine and pure science are peeling
back layers of misunderstanding to reveal patterns of all kinds that could only
be postulated just years ago. We can 'see' the flow of heat through walls, track
our sleep patterns with bracelets or the number of steps we take every day. Our
phones can be used to track and trace our heart rate, our movements through
a city or even the density of communications. A Formula 1 racecar in 2014 had
more than 250 sensors spread throughout it that acquired over 20 MB of data
per lap in each race.[5] This is so much information that teams now create their
own data cloud storage networks to save and manipulate the content. This is an
example of the proliferation of information and communications technology that
has led to a global society that is now more digitally 'connected' than ever.[6] Yet I
would argue this has not led to a more socially connected world. Perhaps when
we reach Ray Kurzweil's projected Singularity[7] in 2050 we will no longer need to
be so connected. Or, perhaps we will speak of the digital cloud having weather as
in the physical world: high and low pressure zones creating turbulent data flows.

On a positive note, the connected world will expose patterns ripe for change.
The profound misuse of water and energy will be revealed and mitigated through
pervasive sensors and computing. I am hopeful that by 2050 those scary, geeky
networks will have evolved into persuasive systems that prompt change.

Steve McCurry

Geisha in the subway

Kyoto

Japan

2007

We will emerge in 2050 intact
if we carry the history and
traditions created before us
into the imaginings of the
future we are creating with our
actions today.

Supply Chain Overhaul

Well-worn supply chains will certainly be disrupted. Since time immemorial, the supply-produce-consume triangle has fuelled economies. It brought slaves to many shores and drove the Industrial Revolution, but over the next 20 years I believe the distance marked in thousands of miles within this triangle will shrivel to double digits. Thus, the teacup I am holding in my hand in California, marked 'Made In England', will certainly be made closer to me in 2050, saving energy and resources. After all, if we can 3D print a kidney today, what will be possible by 2050? Will we be shipping finished products in containers halfway around the world? Or will we have mass-customised small-batch manufacturing in every town? Certainly such a supply chain disruption will challenge current economic power structures.

And since it is looking like it will be a world of greater income equality, we need to remember that history has shown that when an inequality gets too great, nations fall. We need to be mindful of this as we look around the world at countries where the inequality is rapidly increasing or suddenly disappearing.

The economic centre of gravity is a visualisation that charts the historical movement of such power. The centre of that power hovered just north of India and west of China about 2,000 years ago and then slid westward during the Industrial Revolution. While the US is currently the largest GDP producer, by 2050 China will decisively take the lead. By 2025, the centre will have completed its return journey to a point merely 100 kilometres (60 miles) north of where it started.

We need to remember that history has shown that when an inequality gets too great, nations fall

Steve McCurry

Women in a market

Hong Kong

China

1985

The divide between those
who have and those who have
not is erased when it comes
to fresh food and the need to
squeeze a mango yourself.

Elizabeth Gill Lui

Catch of the Day

New Territories

Hong Kong

2005

The biodiversity on offer in a
mobile fish market in Hong
Kong is fresher than anything
one could find prepackaged
in a grocery store. How long
will it last?

Politics is Local

Economic power follows people, and so too will politics of the future. I like to say that politics with a small 'p' speaks of the interaction between people, while politics with a big 'P' refers to the organised boundaries and parties. We are going to see an increased fluidity of political interaction at neighbourhood and city levels because issues are better understood at that level, and when enough people see something being ineffective, smaller systems naturally take over. This is why more city governments have decided to take action on climate change than national governments. While nations spend all their time posturing, cities, with a much closer representational structure, say 'We've got to do something' – and then go out and do it. This kind of action will only increase in the decades to come.

I do believe in the staying power of democracy. But by 2050 we will see the rise of more hybrid systems, as is happening today with the Chinese capitalistic political system or the Russian 'managed democracy' political system. Unrecognisable as a democracy in any textbook from the 1970s, today they seem to be very good at decision-making.

By 2050 we will see the rise of more hybrid systems, as is happening today with the Chinese capitalistic political system

Elizabeth Gill Lui

One World

Wuyishan

China

2006

Young and filled with happiness regardless of the circumstances surrounding them, as long as they have friends and family nearby, our children and our children's children carry the hope we have for a better future.

David Taylor

On the line

Nogales/Mexico

2012

No matter the boundaries – in this case the US border wall on the right, Mexico on the left, and Border Monument No 122 dead centre – children will find a way to make a game of it all. They do not understand the concept of normal. They are born into their own special world. We have the opportunity to rewrite the story that will become the normal they understand.

Notes

1. See the population pyramids of Saudi Arabia, Indonesia and Nigeria, for example: http://populationpyramid.net/.

2. See the population pyramids of Italy, Japan and the US, for example: http://populationpyramid.net/.

3. The Living Planet Index: http://wwf.panda.org/about_our_earth/all_publications/living_planet_report/living_planet_index2/.

4. Kevin Kelly, *What Technology Wants*, Viking (New York), 2010, p 235.

5. Nancy Gohring, 'Tales from the Cloud: How the Lotus F1 Team Builds a Private Cloud for Each Race', CITEWorld, 24 June 2014: www.citeworld.com/article/2366960/big-data-analytics/lotus-f1-team-private-cloud-microsoft-avanade.html.

6. Connected devices surpassed humans on the planet in 2006. See http://medimetrics.com/upload/file/ageofsmrt%20dossier.pdf and www.pcworld.com/article/229170/article.html.

7. The Singularity, a concept championed by computer scientist and futurist Ray Kurzweil, speaks of counting down to the time where Homo sapiens and computation become one (when computing power will match, and then exceed, that of the human brain). Kurzweil has pegged the time right around 2050. In 35 years our computing power will be a billion times more powerful than it is today. A good read might be Ray Kurzweil, *The Age of Intelligent Machines*, MIT Press (Cambridge, MA), 1990.

8. In 2006, with his non-profit organisation Architecture 2030, Mazria issued the 2030 Challenge, a measured and achievable strategy to dramatically reduce global energy consumption and greenhouse gas emissions through low-carbon design. The initiative has since been adopted by the nation's leading professional organisations and architecture firms, influencing the design of billions of square feet of building space worldwide. See http://architecture2030.org.

Steve McCurry

Children play a game of soccer in the streets of Havana

Cuba

2014

This evening ball game on a street in Cuba represents two things: the importance of participation and the critical importance of neighbourhoods. When we are part of something – a team, a neighbourhood, a place – there is great contentment and a sense of freedom to enjoy each other's company.

Designing the New Normal

As a race, there will be countless decisions made as we lurch toward 2050 and beyond. Thankfully we are blessed, we humans, with an endless resourcefulness that dances with our unbridled curiosity. There are many among us who ponder the unthinkable. Brilliant minds, like the neo-futurist architect and systems theorist Richard Buckminster Fuller (1895–1983) or American science-fiction author and professor of biochemistry Isaac Asimov (1920–92), have taken the time to observe, synthesise and dream. They challenged the status quo of what was, and dared to think and create the unthinkable. Their work challenges each one of us to stop, listen to our inner voices and create the best versions of ourselves that we can be.

Our job as a community of designers – one that I believe carries a significant weight for the success of all things big and small on planet Earth – is to acknowledge that issues must be engaged through all of the STEEP lenses and then to galvanise action, just as founder and CEO Edward Mazria has done with Architecture 2030.[8] It is an opportunity – and an obligation. If we look at all the issues before us with an objective and clear mind, as we would any design problem, we can contextualise for the world that is coming. We can redirect positively. I invite you to help co-create a future that we desire; to evolve the new normal we need in order to thrive as we arrive at 2050. ᴆ

Chris Luebkeman

A Conversation with Design Luminary Paola Antonelli

Designing a Graceful Ending

Still from Fritz Lang's
Metropolis

1927

The suffering and bleak vision of the future, as imagined by the film's director. The urban dystopia of Lang's science-fiction classic set in a futuristic city sharply divided between the working classes and wealthy industrialists was influenced by the work of the Italian architect Antonio Sant'Elia and the skyscrapers of New York City.

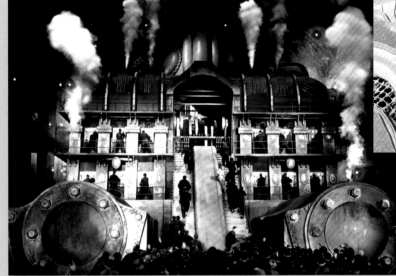

To ask Paola Antonelli what the future of design will be is to ask her the wrong question. This is because for Antonelli, Senior Curator of the Department of Architecture and Design and Director of Research and Development at the Museum of Modern Art (MoMA) in New York, design is not an event to be anticipated, but rather a tool to build the future. 'One of my favorite refrains is that design helps people deal with change,' she states. 'In the future there will be dramatic changes, just like in the past and in the present, and design will be there to transform these revolutions into real life.' Antonelli redirects the question simply, by identifying the push and pull inherent in design: 'Design is in the service of progress and is also a fundamental engine for progress.'

She observes that our future has been imagined and reimagined with great spectacle and intensity, usually portrayed as either a utopia, 'gleaming white, translucent, perfect and spick and span', or as a dystopian, dark and dirty dimension, riddled with vice and suffering, in the tradition of Fritz Lang's *Metropolis* (1927) or Ridley Scott's *Blade Runner* (1982). While creative, these two polar visions are short on reality. The world is seldom black or white, and nor are the parameters of life on earth. 'What does change is culture, our understanding of how the world evolves. We make mistakes, achieve successes, we learn (hopefully), technology advances, values shift. We call it progress, and this is the designer's domain.'

Terreform ONE

Super Docking

Brooklyn Navy Yards

New York

2014

The future is often envisioned as a perfectly organised utopia, just like this theoretical white, latticed monolithic structure emerging from an urban industrial site in Brooklyn, as envisioned by Mitchell Joachim and Terreform ONE.

In his bid to discover how design might shape the future, Guest-Editor **Chris Luebkeman** went to speak to **Paola Antonelli**, Senior Curator of the Department of Architecture and Design and Director of Research and Development at the Museum of Modern Art (MoMA) in New York. A passionate advocate of the power of design, Antonelli describes to Luebkeman how design can be a fundamental tool for the future, having the potential to intercede with empathy and a human touch between raw new technological advances and future users, rendering innovative technologies useable and accessible, and ultimately enabling a graceful and poetic end to the world as we know it.

Progress By Design

Antonelli illustrates design in the service of progress by raising the introduction of the Internet to the wider world in the early 1990s. In the beginning the Internet was, for most of us, difficult to understand and even more difficult to use, as it was made up of lines of code. Its awesome potential was there, but it was inaccessible to most because it lacked clarity and legibility. The work of interface designers changed this, in part. The 1993 Mosaic interface, which later flowed into Netscape, was the first 'intuitive' interface to make the World Wide Web and the Internet accessible to laypeople. 'When Mosaic came, with its buttons, windows and hyperlinks, all of a sudden everybody with a computer and the right cabling could use the Internet,' she explains. It was only when the Internet made sense to the human mind that it truly became useful. Marc Andreessen and his team at the University of Illinois National Center for Supercomputing Applications (NCSA) opened it up to the world. As Antonelli points out, however, even today the Internet remains inaccessible to nearly 60 per cent of the world's population.[1] Design can also help in this contemporary challenge.

As Antonelli underlines, designers have always played a key role in the challenges that will change the way we go about our daily lives, and will continue to do so in the future: 'Designers make innovations manageable and approachable, so that they can be embraced and assimilated into life. And they never forget functionality and elegance.' As self-driving cars are introduced, for example, the idea of ceding control of the driving experience to a machine will be inherently awkward and disempowering for many. Antonelli believes design will soften the blow: 'Engineers will figure out the schematics, scientists will perfect the cars' swarm intelligence, and mechanics will build them. But it will be the designers who will allay our fears. It will be designers who will allow the self-driving cars to flirt with our imagination, race through our fantasies, and still let us feel safe. It will be a design-build team that will make us trust the machine, that will humanise the new system.'

Dunne & Raby

Designs For An Overpopulated
Planet: Foragers

2009

A look at how humans might in 2050 wrest control of their personal food production through evolutionary processes and molecular technologies of a planet with increased population, limited natural resources and climate challenges.

The Human Touch

For Antonelli, humanity is at the core of design's scope. Keeping this central preoccupation in mind, 'the most promising designers build teams,' she clarifies. 'They have knowledge of a particular aspect of design, and they are conversant in the languages spoken by other specialists who they will need to involve to achieve their goals. Since they have a real interest in human beings, they try to marry the deepest human needs with the most progressive tools. I am always looking for designers who are able to take into account the most advanced technology, but also able to join it with tradition. I think that today, the best approach towards the future incorporates certain fundamental, necessary elements of the past. Design does not always need to be disruptive, never-seen-before and alienating.'

She has recently added works by designers including Tomáš Gabzdil Libertíny (*The Honeycomb Vase 'Made by Bees'*, 2006) and Markus Kayser (*Solar-sintered Bowl*, 2011) to MoMA's collection, and looks to the Dutch industrial designer Hella Jongerius and her interplay between new technology and handmade crafts.

'I admire designers who are able to take inspiration and experience from local culture, from the interaction between old and new, and high-tech and low-tech, and bring all these ingredients together so that though the objects and experiences they create might have been designed with the most advanced technology, they feel like they are already a part of our lives.'

Theoretical Design Explorers

Antonelli envisions that the future potential for design to elevate humanity is immense. She also sees a bifurcation that will send design into uncharted territory: 'Design will go the way of physics: I like to think that there will be applied designers and theoretical designers.' Applied design will carry on the mission of shaping the objects and experiences of our lives. The theoretical designers will be explorers and they will take their humanistic design education and proficiency and apply them to fields that have not traditionally been their domain, such as politics, economics and sociology, to help shape the culture and infrastructures that govern our societies.

Markus Kayser

Solar-sintered Bowl

2011

Kayser is interested in the use of natural resources in 3D printing, a counterintuitive step in a technology that is so closely identified with computers, robotics and synthetic resins. Experiments with solar power led him to the desert environment and the two elements most readily available there: sun and sand, the silica component of which solidifies as glass when heated to a melting point and allowed to cool.

We could design a much sweeter ending for ourselves, and think responsibly of the species that will survive the human race

Ren Ri

Honeycomb Sculptures

T Museum

Hangzhou, China

2010

An ironic counterpoint to rapid industrial manufacturing techniques, Beijing-based artist Ren Ri has developed a strategy that turns the hive's beeswax into semi-calculated sculptures that study the interaction between humans and nature.

Twitter message

London 2012 Olympic Games Opening Ceremony

London

2012

'This is for everyone'. The British computer scientist Tim Berners-Lee, inventor of the World Wide Web, lit up the London 2012 Olympic stadium with this Twitter message. His buoyant tweet highlighted the way that the Internet – perhaps the most radical social design experiment of the last quarter century – has created seemingly limitless possibilities for discovering, sharing and expanding knowledge and information.

Why shouldn't we design better systems for social justice all around the world? How can design inform domestic policy? What would international diplomacy look like if designers thought deeply about it?, she asks, rhetorically. 'Because of their human-centred approach and their attention to goals and means, I see designers as having a crucial role in society; design has a very tangible constructive potential, even in its most speculative forms.'

A Graceful Ending

Design can help us construct, but it is also part of the ultimate endgame. When Antonelli speaks about the future of humankind in an age where we are contemplating the extinction of species that could include our own, she envisions that design 'will help us become extinct more gracefully, at least. I don't know if we'll be able to stop the process that we have set in motion, but at least we can do it with a little more poetry.'

With candour, she illuminates that the meaning in her life and work as a curator of design comes from and revolves around the other people around her: 'I really believe that design and architecture are the highest forms of creative expression that human beings have. They relate to people's lives in very direct manner. It is a great responsibility.'

Perhaps one of the best gifts Antonelli can imagine designers giving to the future of the human race is a greater capacity for empathy: 'A future left in the hands of a designer would be a future of compassion and of elegance with a certain degree of sadness because I think that most designers know where we're headed. But there is also hope. We could design a much sweeter ending for ourselves, and think responsibly of the species that will survive the human race.' ⌂

The article is based on a conversation between Chris Luebkeman and Paola Antonelli in her office at MoMA, New York, on 3 October 2014

Alexandra Daisy Ginsberg

Designing for the Sixth Extinction

2013

Some scientists believe, given the accelerated loss of species and natural ecosystems in the present, that the earth is currently experiencing the next widespread extinction in the history of biology. Ginsberg's speculative project attempts to reverse-engineer the damage humans have caused to the planet, designing synthetic organisms to 'rewild' our environment and re-create newly sustainable biodiverse landscapes.

Note   1. www.internetlivestats.com/internet-users/ based on information from www.itu.int/net/pressoffice/ press_releases/2014/23.aspx#.VOo1prDF8ww.

Concept art for *Minority Report*

20th Century Fox

2002

The creative team imagined that a massive
influx of population drawn by the precogs'
influence on creating a murder-free society
had given rise to a vast vertical city across the
Potomac River. In this immensely vertical, future
Washington DC, vehicles might be required to
negotiate vertical space as well as horizontal.
This illustration by artist Darek Gogal shows
three-dimensional roadways that have therefore
become a necessity, extrapolated forward
from the combination of the elevator and the
driverless car.

PREJUDICIAL NARRATIVES

Film production requires world building: the power to visualise and bring to life narrative through a film's total environment. This is often entirely speculative, imagining alternative or future worlds. Here, **Alex McDowell**, acclaimed British production designer, producer and Professor at the University of Southern California (USC) describes his world-building, narrative approach to production design, which he consolidated in the Steven Spielberg film *Minority Report* (2002) that envisioned Washington DC in the year 2050. The possibilities of this storytelling technique are demonstrated by its transference into real-life projects, such as the immersive model that his production company, 5D GlobalStudio, developed for Al Baydha, a Bedouin village in Saudi Arabia.

ALEX
MCDOWELL

BUILDING TOMORROW'S WORLD TODAY

—

In 1895, Raymond Lao wrecks his merchant ship and washes up on the shores of an isolated atoll in the middle of the Pacific. Taken in by local inhabitants, he observes them using a remarkable fuel source for heat: the sap of the indigenous muka tree. Raymond realises that the tree is rhizomic and deduces an enormous fuel source below the island in its roots. He founds the Lao Oil Company, and the island's population explodes. In a short number of years, this multicultural society evolves into the archipelago of Rilao. Soon the Lao Oil Company threatens the world fossil-fuel industries, and a mysterious plague and imposed quarantine permanently close Rilao's borders. The archipelago quickly disappears from maps until the turn of the millennium, when the island is rediscovered and gradually begins to reveal its complex parallel universe.

This entirely fictional world of Rilao was created in January 2014. Architect Ann Pendleton-Jullian and I developed it as the basis for a world building course at the University of Southern California (USC) School of Cinematic Arts in Los Angeles. Our intent was to seed a rich fictive yet grounded world with the fewest number of inceptive cues. We started the semester by imagining a city formed from the chance encounter of the DNAs of Rio de Janeiro and LA, placed on a small island in the Pacific that was too small for its growing population. This simple prompt stimulated a range of complex narratives from a cross-disciplinary group of undergraduate, graduate and PhD students that included filmmakers, game makers, industrial designers, engineers, architects and writers.

The world's rich inherent logic allowed for highly complex story development; in turn Rilao has a coherence grounded in reality, taking real constraints (gravity, weather, geography, poverty, family) and using these to allow a fictional world to evolve independently. Within world building spaces, one can prototype the

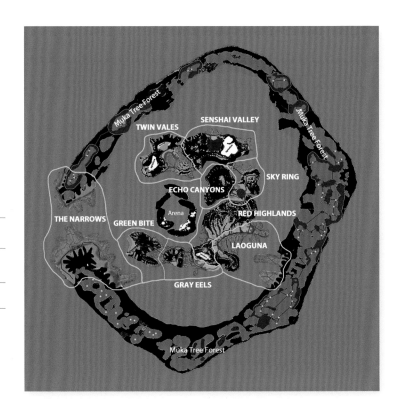

Lauren Fenton and Eric Marshall/
World Building Media Lab

Map of Rilao

University of Southern California (USC)
School of Cinematic Arts

Los Angeles, California

2014

This open-source and persistent world building project imagined a fictional archipelago in the Pacific with a population that has expanded beyond the constraint of the landmass. A unique fuel source, a plague, an extensive terraforming game and an embargo that removed the atoll from the maps of the real world are some of the narrative triggers for more than 100 student projects and over 1,000 stories developed by students and professionals from several countries through the USC World Building Media Lab and World Building Institute joint project.

'what if?' and 'why not?' – and these interrogations stimulate new narratives into existence. Simple questions demanded of the world – 'What if television was never invented', or 'What architecture might result from massive overcrowding in a bounded set of islands?' – trigger a compelling investigation that results in new thinking, stories and artefacts.

Although Rilao was largely developed to investigate the future, it was necessary to first create deep history, mythology, socio-politics and infrastructure that would evolve a world intuitively and provide a narrative foundation from which hundreds of stories would emerge. There is a mutual agreement between the multiple authors in building a collaborative world that the logic evolves responsively. Since its inception, the world of Rilao has become the subject for design fiction at the Royal Collage of Art in London (Design Interactions course led by professors Fiona Raby and Tony Dunne) and Hogeschool Rotterdam University (Gamification course led by Professor Bruno Setola); as part of an investigation by journalists at the ESBM School in Rio (led by professors João Luiz de Figueiredo Silva and Pedro Curi); and in the work of the USC School of Architecture and the Bauhaus (with Professors Neil Leach and Alexander Kalachev); and a full year of projects in the USC Media Arts + Practice world building classes.

All of these projects contributed to a vast collaborative one-day world build with 240 participants at the USC World Building Institute's 'Science of Fiction' event in October 2014. The event was facilitated by myself and co-curated with USC Professor Jeff Watson, who created the Rilao Remote Viewing Protocol – a card game that aided in the generation of over a thousand stories within Rilao in a single day.

From this vast and fertile ground, many of the Rilaoan narratives evolved into imaginings of future politics and society, the implications of a national plague on science and culture, and on the psyche of the nation; terraforming techniques for land growth and new architectural solutions to counter the impact of overpopulation; the development of language and storytelling; and new religion and mythology.

The fulfilment of building any unrealised world is to see how specific prompts can incept a vast and complex series of intersecting logic points whose call and response provoke decussating ripples that originate from the individual triggers like pebbles dropped into still water, and quickly become a complex set of patterns that form the rationale of a new and coherent world. A broad horizontal knowledge of the world develops systematically while deep vertical core narratives continuously test the world and make it increasingly robust.

In 1999, with the new millennium providing a focus for films like *Fight Club*, which I designed with a dystopian view of a blank generation future that tied right back into my punk years as a music industry designer, I was invited by Steven Spielberg to production design a film of the Philip K Dick story *Minority Report* (1956). In order for the film's futuristic narrative to have exigent impact for its audience, Spielberg wanted to approach the film with the lens of future reality, not science fiction. The setting was Washington DC, in the year 2050. Beyond this place and time the film's creative team had very little other information, and the paucity of a scripted narrative led us instinctively to a world building process that has become the foundation of my continuing design practice.

A film does not usually begin pre-production until a script is nominally in place, but for *Minority Report* the writer Scott Frank and I began work on the same day. Without any script in place I had to take a different approach to defining the story context. The production designer's first task is to create the design language that defines the distinct, visual rules of the film. This time, instead of deriving this from the text, we sculpted the language out of a few narrative triggers from the director – the time and place, the broad intent of this story to develop a world

Behnaz Farahi/
World Building Media Lab

Camouflage

University of Southern California
(USC) School of Cinematic Arts

Los Angeles, California

2014

Citizens of Rilao endow themselves with the sophisticated mechanical limbs pictured here that they control through muscular movements. The structure moves autonomously in sympathy with the gestures of the wearer, speaking to issues of display and privacy in an overpopulated city.

from the ground up, and the three precognitive beings at the centre of this world, known as the precogs, as the central disruptor.

We took the broad horizontal slice through the world based on acquiring knowledge, and from this developed a 'bible' that defined the primary logic drivers for the film's vision. We spent time with a diverse group of domain experts led by futurist Peter Schultz and including quantum physicist Neil Gershenfeld and architect Bill Mitchell from the MIT Media Lab, art science pioneer Jaron Lanier, writer Doug Copeland, journalist Joel Garreau, Dr Shaun Jones from the Defense Advanced Research Projects Agency (DARPA) and others. Spielberg, Scott Frank and I, along with our team, had a fascinating immersion in the stimulating tension between the anticipated future of the futurist group and the directed future of the storytellers.

In the course of the film, we developed a new system for stimulating and unfolding a narrative world. For example, from the fictional precogs at the core of the storyworld, who can predict impending murder, we imagined that a desire for a murder-free society would stimulate a population to migrate to the precogs' sphere of influence. This influx would result in rapid urban development of a vertical infrastructure and a unique transportation system, which in turn became one trigger for the narrative. This development of core logic that creates specific lenses to extrapolate

forward into rich emergent narrative became our world building process.

This is prejudicial storytelling – a mediated framework for the world one is developing, while remaining entirely open to the subtle changes that evolve directly from the fabric of this created world. The horizontal slice that diagnoses the intended future world defines the broad vision, while through a series of vertical 'core samples' one tests the fine detail of that world in relation to the story. This knowledge applies directly to core elements of the story, and each dive either strengthens or decays the organic logic that is scaffolding the world. In *Minority Report* we could determine at any point along the journey the possibilities for a protagonist who elects to turn left instead of right, defining an enormously resourceful world in advance of it locking into a linear script.

This evolutionary design development provided the depth that the film needed to immerse the audience in a vision that included precognition, a murder-free society and the essential loss of civil liberties at the heart of the story. Through deep research we were able to create the iconic vision of consumer targeting, gesture recognition, driverless cars, personal devices and quantum mechanics for precognition, and develop an integrated vision that has resulted in over 100 patents in the years since the film's release. The film has become proof of the ability for a

Still from *Minority Report*

20th Century Fox

2002

Scientist John Underkoffler collaborated with Alex McDowell and the creative team on *Minority Report* to develop a gesture-based system for Tom Cruise's character. This fictional prototype of gesture recognition was developed into a real-world interface called G-Speak by Underkoffler and his start-up Oblong company after the film was released.

Alex McDowell

World Building Mandala

2014

The 21st-century digital and non-linear world building design process replaces the anachronism of the linear, industrial 20th-century model and allows for a fluid cross-disciplinary collaboration from the start of the development of the story space.

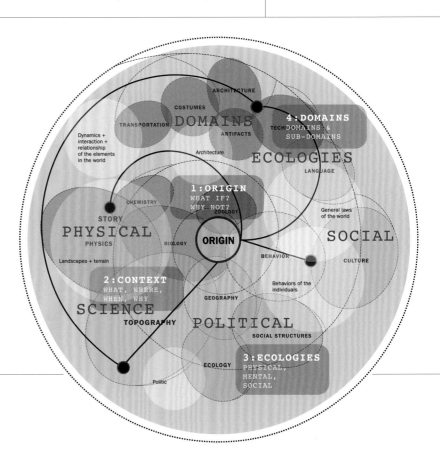

Concept art for *Minority Report*

20th Century Fox

2002

Much of the design of the precog chamber in Steven Spielberg's film was prompted by physicist Neil Gershenfeld's proposition of quantum entanglement as the mechanic for precognition. Using a ripple pattern on the walls suggested both the narrative metaphor and insulation for the minds of the precogs.

Concept art for *Minority Report*

20th Century Fox

2002

By conducting research with a wealth of experts in architecture, engineering, science, urban planning, technology and advertising, Alex McDowell and his team of domain experts on the film developed a logic-driven informed vision of the near future. Brand strategy and consumer experience expert Anne White consulted on the interactive, customised, location-responsive marketing that was woven throughout the film, as demonstrated by this concept art by Mark Goerner.

By completely immersing ourselves in the development of the world, world builders are simultaneously both creator and first user. Non-linear, creative collaborative development paired with interactive technologies and multiple lenses characterises world building.

world-framed narrative to not only envision the future, but also to instigate it.

As a different example of applying world building in the real world, we can look to Al Baydha, a village development 60 kilometres (40 miles) south of Mecca in Saudi Arabia. On the ground, this sustainability project will generate new architecture and agriculture for a Bedouin population of 3,000 tribesfolk. In a region where rain falls once every three years, creating flash floods that traditionally destroyed any possibility of sustained farming, the villagers have begun a process of permaculture that captures the sparse rainfall and regenerates the soil.

What was missing in Al Baydha was an accessible and truthful expression of the long-term vision. 5D GlobalStudio engaged a small team of programmers and designers to develop a typology and system for a precognitive view of the progress of the village and land, in a virtual, immersive and interactive model. By carefully constructing a future world from the exact specifications and rules of the culture, history, society, terrain and climate, we can accurately

predict a fully functioning village over the next 10 years. Through careful modelling, lighting, texture and sound we blend art and science to offer back to the stakeholders – the Bedouin villagers themselves – a fully expanded vision to which they can subscribe and that they can own.

These three different applications of world building highlight its adaptability and practical use as the basis of a new design and storytelling practice. World building takes on a range of multi-platform tools and capabilities and engages them with narrative so that multiple 'actors' can collaborate across disciplines in real time. By completely immersing ourselves in the development of the world, world builders are simultaneously both creator and first user. Non-linear, creative collaborative development paired with interactive technologies and multiple lenses characterises world building. This volatile creative process, applied fluidly to a broad spectrum of media and environments to intuit and construct logic pathways, delivers a lucid vision of near-real, parallel and fictional worlds. ∆

Al–Baydha Project

Mecca, Saudia Arabia

2014–

An immersive communications tool, the Al Baydha Project involved a completely virtual world build of a Bedouin village in a desert. Built by 5D GlobalStudio, this predictive virtual world is not a game or an animated film, but an interactive tool to experience how traditional culture and new technologies weave together in an accurate projection of future reality.

Chris Luebkeman

Design Is Our Answer

An Interview with Leading Design Thinker Tim Brown

What do the Apple mouse and the stand-up toothpaste tube share in common? They were both developed by IDEO, the global design and innovation firm led by CEO and President **Tim Brown**. Guest-Editor **Chris Luebkeman** met with Brown to find out about the possibilities of human-centred design thinking.

IDEO President and CEO, Tim Brown.

The next time you touch the mouse on your computer, say a little 'thank you' to the concept of human-centred design and innovation championed by a design firm born in the heart of the Silicon Valley of California. Indeed, the 'Age of IDEO' will be looked upon by future generations as a turning point in the role of design in contemporary life.

Founded in 1991 in Palo Alto, California,[1] IDEO believed that the only way towards brilliant design was by having deep empathy for the consumer. They observed humans, talked to them, sat with them, and studied their behaviour. Then their teams of designers, engineers and scientists, linguists, psychologists, biologists, teachers, artists and philosophers got to brainstorming and building together.

They embraced the term 'design thinking', a human-centred approach to innovation that draws from the designer's toolkit to integrate the needs of people, the possibilities of technology, and the requirements for business success. It is this kind of thinking that will bring us successfully into, and through, the challenges of the next decades. As Sir Ken Robinson so eloquently points out: 'What you're doing now, or have done in the past, need not determine what you can do next and in the future.' And it is that future which Tim Brown, President and CEO of IDEO, has his eyes on.[2]

Layered Thinking

For Brown, the design thinking process is best thought of as a system of overlapping spaces – inspiration, ideation and implementation – rather than a sequence of orderly steps. Inspiration is the problem or opportunity that motivates the search for solutions. Ideation is the process of generating, developing and testing ideas. Implementation is the path that leads from the project stage into people's lives.

'At IDEO at least, better together is a fundamental business strategy,' he explains. 'It brings together what is desirable from a human point of view with what is technologically feasible and economically viable. It allows people who are not trained as designers to use creative tools to address a vast range of challenges, and embrace wild ideas during brainstorming.'

Out of such unique thinking sprung the original Apple mouse, the stand-up toothpaste tube, a talking portable heart defibrillator and a better classroom chair. Iconic companies such as Procter & Gamble, PepsiCo, Steelcase and Ford have IDEO on speed dial.

Indeed, Brown has spoken to Ivy League universities about the prospect of design thinking becoming a core liberal art along with such staples as history, literature and philosophy. He believes it may be considered so elemental to education in the near future that it will be consciously integrated into the primary schools curriculum along with reading, writing and arithmetic.

Democratising Design

IDEO's immense success has hinged on freeing design from the binds that have constrained the practice for centuries. Instead of the power of design sitting upstream, in the hands of a few people working behind closed doors, IDEO democratised it. They wanted ideas from everyone. They saw the value, and profit, of inclusion.

What student of design or innovation doesn't remember the video demonstrating the design process of IDEO's new shopping cart concept aired on ABC's 'Nightline' news programme in 1999?[3] Its clear illustration of the Deep Dive became mandatory viewing. Tasked with creating a better shopping cart, IDEO brought together their internal team of thinkers, studied the problem from all angles by talking to all stakeholders, pitched wild ideas internally, refined the best ones, and created a modular and safer model.

At Your Service

When Brown, an industrial designer who joined the firm in 1994, took the helm at the turn of the century, IDEO was an established product design firm making expressive and impressive products. However, while working in the UK, his product clients were slowly being replaced by services clients. This demonstrated to him that 'experience design' – really using smart design to improve services – was a viable new route for the firm, and revealed design's potential for creative problem-solving in both commercial and organisational contexts. This idea was new to Silicon Valley, and it pushed IDEO in a new direction.

IDEO,
First production mouse
for Lisa and Macintosh,
1980

The IDEO-developed mouse for Apple's radical new computer, the Lisa. Its simplicity, functionality and low fabrication cost made it an instant success.

They embraced the term 'design thinking', a human-centred approach to innovation

IDEO,
Redesign of the
shopping cart,
ABC 'Nightline',
1999

IDEO was asked to demonstrate its process for innovation for an episode of ABC's late-night news show 'Nightline'. This still from the programme illustrated IDEO's new shopping cart concept, which considered issues such as manoeuvrability, shopping behaviour, child safety and maintenance cost. The multidisciplinary team were recorded as they brainstormed, researched, prototyped and gathered user feedback for a design that went from idea to working model in four days.

OpenIDEO Global
problem-solving
platform,
2014

OpenIDEO is an open innovation
platform to help solve social
impact-based challenges in
a global context.

IDEO offices,
Chicago,
2013

Building prototypes is part
of every designer's job.

IDEO open-plan workspaces,
San Francisco,
California,
2014

The open-plan layout
allows for both planned and
serendipitous collaboration.

Collaborations sprung up with the most unlikely partners. Thanks to the Sara and Evan Williams Foundation, IDEO worked with the San Francisco Unified School District's food services in 2013 to help redefine the lunchtime experience for students. There was a clear case of systemic dissatisfaction with the quality of the food, and even after Revolutionary Foods, a group known to serve some of the highest nutritional meals in the nation, was brought in, the children still chose not to eat at school. As IDEO discovered after working with 1,300 students, parents, union leaders, nutrition staff, board commissioners, principals and teachers, the reason wasn't the food, but the lack of an eating experience. Changing the experience based on what the children respond to has changed the outcome.

IDEO also turned their attention to the role of the librarian and the reading room in 2013. With the sponsorship of the Bill & Melinda Gates Foundation, the Chicago Public Library and Denmark's Aarhus Public Libraries worked together with IDEO to evolve and adapt the role of the typically quiet bricks-and-mortar library to users' changing needs in the digital information age. The resulting Design Thinking Toolkit for Libraries[4] offers reading and workshop materials that propose, among other things, teen expression labs with music- and art-making tools, a tech spa for users looking for 'how to' information, and narrative storytelling workshops for children.

By focusing on the service element, Brown was determined to become an important voice for the potential of design in the business community. IDEO became one of the initial members of the World Economic Forum's community of New Champions in 2007 when he attended the inaugural event in Tianjin, China. This group is considered to be the next generation of fast-growing enterprises shaping the future of business and society together with leaders from major multinationals as well as government, media, academia and civil society. Brown was one of the first members of the Forum's design council. He is now focused on expanding this influence by encouraging the concept of global collaboration through OpenIDEO,[5] a global, online community that offers challenges or calls to action around social issues. Students, artists and iconoclasts, labourers and visionaries now have an open invitation to join together to help solve some of the challenges facing the world today.

Architects can reimagine themselves and their profession as something greater; not merely the designers of buildings, but designers of systems.

Architects Making the Jump
Brown sees the world of architecture as poised to make similar changes. He believes architects can reimagine themselves and their profession as something greater; not merely the designers of buildings, but designers of systems.

Perhaps it is impossible for many to separate the field of architecture from the practice, but this is what Brown feels is holding so many professionals within self-determined constraints. 'Architectural education is the best systems design education in the world. There's a reason why we hire lots of architects – not because they want to be architects or we want to do buildings, but because they're wonderful systems designers. This is why I love architects.'

And yet the true value of an architect lies in his or her ability to create a solution for unique sets of circumstances. As Brown explains: 'The power that designers have in the world is through their understanding of how to make things real. A deep, innate understanding of what is needed to make things is actually a very important part of design thinking.' The products of architecture – the order and structure, the beauty and the grandeur, the safety and the stability, the unity and the legacy – have been cherished by civilisation. 'It has made a difference to society for thousands of years and there's no reason why it shouldn't in the future.'

But, he explains, there is a catch. If the field of architecture is to remain relevant, it must focus more on the meaning and less on the mechanisms of the trade.

'I would encourage architectural students to think about the difference between practising architectural design and practising the profession of architecture.' He points to the way in which design tools have become democratised. 'An analysis that required a room of humans bent over tables just one generation ago is now executed in microseconds at the push of a button. Rendering techniques that took years of apprenticeship to master are now found in a pull-down menu by any 12-year-old with the proper software. Even the tools needed to design and procure a building may soon be available to those without an architecture degree.'

Move Over Humans
Or – gasp – even a heartbeat.

Brown sees the vitality of technology-driven design adumbrated in the fields of data and software where technology and algorithms are capable of designing for themselves. 'The history of technology has been that eventually it gets approachable enough that less technological people, in other words designers, can kind of wrap their arms around it and start to do something interesting with it.' And, as he points out, examples of how tech-driven design could fit into the big picture already exist.

'Chip design is an interesting parallel. Chip design used to be very smart engineers drawing lines on film, and then eventually lines on 2D CAD systems, and then the computers took over. There is hardly a human hand that touches the design of chips these days. Specifications go in one end and chip designs come out at the other. It's all driven by machines, and so there are no more chip designers in the kind of conventional sense of the word.'

With a core vision centred around affordability, scalability and excellence, IDEO collaborated with the Innova team to build a school from the ground up. After months of fieldwork and prototyping, the curriculum, teaching strategies, buildings, operational plans, and underlying financial model to run the network of schools in Peru were developed. The Media Lab here is a key part of the Innova experience, and is placed right at the entrance to Innova's Chimbote campus.

IDEO,
Innova Schools,
Chimbote,
Peru,
2012

Innova's cafeteria extends into the courtyard, and can be used for project-based learning throughout the day.

IDEO collaborated with the Innova team to devise the school's core methodology and curriculum. Here, an internal courtyard displays the key elements of the learning model highlighted for students and community members.

'Solo learning' through technology in one of Innova's multi-modal classrooms. Pairs of classrooms are divided by a sliding wall, which when closed creates two small-format classes for 30 students. When open, two classrooms become one large-format space tailored for technology-enabled learning for up to 60 students.

Design is capable of solving far more complex problems – problems with solutions that have the potential to lift not only individual lives, but all of us collectively as a society and a civilisation.

Embracing Complex Issues

'Now that some of the tradition-bound limits on how we should think about design have been removed, we are free to not just allow, but to encourage design to permeate deeper and far more broadly than ever.' Design is the process itself and, as Brown puts it, 'design has proliferated into everything'.

He believes design is capable of solving far more complex problems – problems with solutions that have the potential to lift not only individual lives, but all of us collectively as a society and a civilisation. While these problems are intricate, subtle, pervasive and stubborn, that doesn't bother Brown one bit. He would like design to be used to combat climate change. And pervasive poverty. He dares to imagine that design might have a role in ending war.

While these problems are far too complex for any individual to get very far with, an institution or a league of institutions with teams of highly proficient, educated design thinkers would be able to find clever ways to leap from today's advances to tomorrow's solutions.

'The future I've picked for IDEO,' says Brown, 'will allow the kind of openness of design to happen and at the same time focus our efforts on some of the most difficult challenges we can find.' His grand vision casts us – the entire human family – as the beneficiaries of the power of good design. ⌀

The article is based on a conversation between Chris Luebkeman and Tim Brown in IDEO's San Francisco office on 23 September 2014.

Notes
1. IDEO was created by a merger of the established design firms of David Kelley Design (founded by Stanford University professor David Kelley), London-based Moggridge Associates and San Francisco's ID Two (both founded by British-born Bill Moggridge), and Matrix Product Design (founded by Mike Nuttall).
2. Dan Schawbel, 'Sir Ken Robinson: How to Discover Your True Talents', Forbes, 5 June 2013: www.forbes.com/sites/danschawbel/2013/06/05/sir-ken-robinson-how-to-discover-your-true-talents/.
3. www.youtube.com/watch?v=M66ZU2PCIcM.
4. http://designthinkingforlibraries.com/.
5. https://openideo.com/.

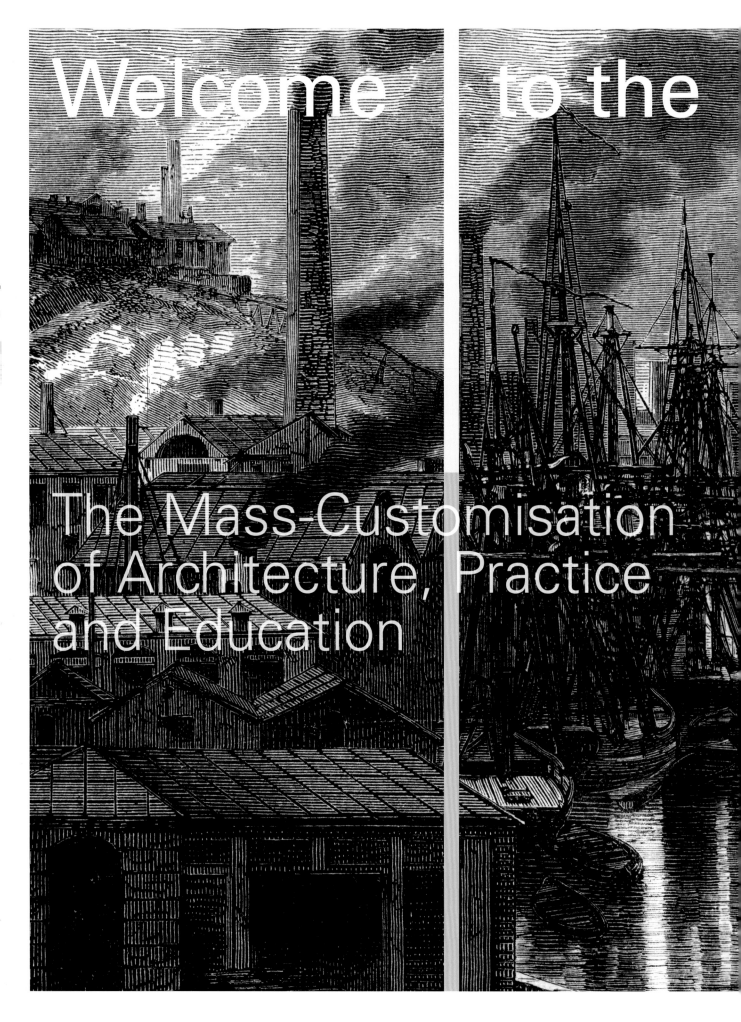

Welcome to the

The Mass-Customisation of Architecture, Practice and Education

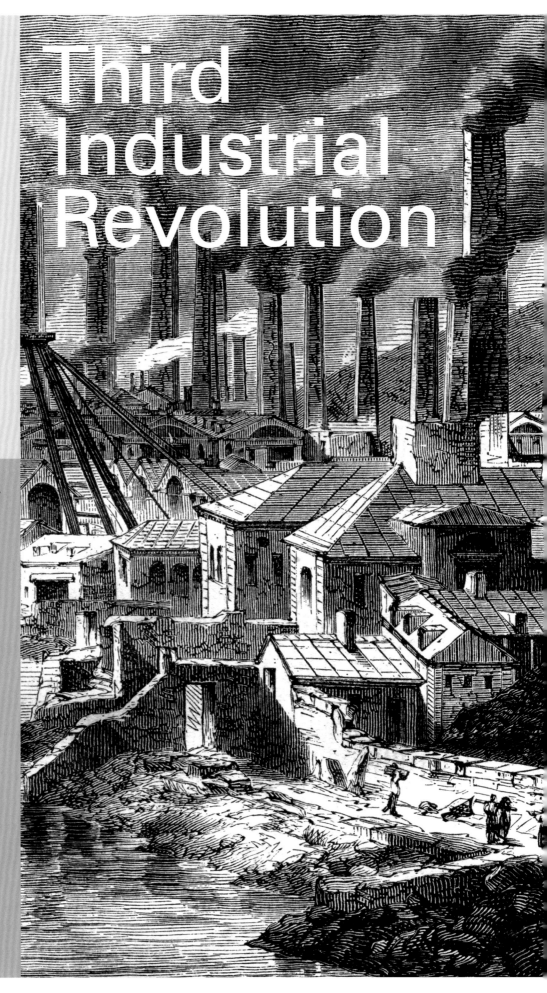

Thomas Fisher

Third Industrial Revolution

First Industrial
Revolution, 19th century

The steam engine allowed the
mechanisation of hand labour.
Pollution from copper factories
in Cornwall, England.

Engraving from *History of
England* by Rollins, 1887.

In 2050, the built environment and the practice of architecture will have changed exponentially. The influential writer and editor **Thomas Fisher**, a Professor at the School of Architecture and Dean of the College of Design at the University of Minnesota, explains the impact of the Third Industrial Revolution on architecture, and how it will lead to self-generated mass customisation, coupled with a denser sustainable, urban form. Responding to this context, architects will need to become highly collaborative 'design strategists, bringing together whatever disciplines clients need to help them achieve their organisational goals.'

By 2050, the Third Industrial Revolution will be well underway and with it will come dramatic changes in the practice of architecture and in architecture itself. As with the First Industrial Revolution of the 19th century, in which we mechanised hand labour, and the Second Industrial Revolution of the 20th century, when assembly lines replaced stationary construction, the Third Industrial Revolution will bring a shift away from the mass production and mass consumption of the last 100 years, towards an economy based on mass customisation. Digitally based technologies will allow people to 3D print, laser cut and CNC fabricate not just consumer goods, but also the parts and even the whole of buildings.

This will disrupt many of the relationships and alter many of the practices that have characterised the building industry over the last two centuries. The now-clear distinction between producer and consumer will blur as owner-builders increasingly construct their own environments. And the moving of building materials and products around the globe, as we do now, will become much less common as technology facilitates the local fabrication of goods, enhancing the competitiveness of local economies.

This may seem contrary to the world as we know it, one in which global companies and the global economy have dominated local ones. But as happened in the previous two Industrial Revolutions, the apparent invincibility of a system marks the point of its greatest vulnerability and the moment in which it stands poised to fall. We know that the dependence on fossil fuels makes our current system unsustainable, and by 2050 the reality of that will have completely transformed the ways in which we live and work.

FIRST INDUSTRIAL REVOLUTION

Machine-made goods

SECOND INDUSTRIAL REVOLUTION

Assembly line mass production

THIRD INDUSTRIAL REVOLUTION

Self-generated mass customisation

The moving of
building materials
and products around
the globe, as we do
now, will become
much less common

Mass-Customised Cities and Buildings

At the urban scale, we will see the gradual disappearance of sprawling, disaggregated cities. Instead of separate residential and commercial districts, with large-scale manufacturing and big-box retailing in their own single-use zones, we will see a reintegration of living, working and making in the same districts and even, as happened before the First Industrial Revolution, on the same block or site. This has already begun to happen in cities, as denser, mixed-use communities arise to accommodate new economic activity and as ever greater numbers of people work from home or live within walking or biking distance of their jobs.

Architecture will change accordingly. Along with single-use zoning will go single-use buildings, replaced by highly flexible structures able to adjust to residential, commercial and light-manufacturing uses with minimal change. Such buildings will have durable, adaptable structures with easily reusable or biodegradable interior fit-outs. They will also generate much of their own solar, wind and/or geothermal power, with district utility systems supplying the rest. The collaborative nature of the Third Industrial Revolution will lead building owners and inhabitants to recycle what they can no longer use and share what they cannot make or generate themselves.

The Disaggregated City of the Second Industrial Revolution maximised mass production and consumption.

The Re-aggregated City of the Third Industrial Revolution will maximise the connectedness needed for mass customisation.

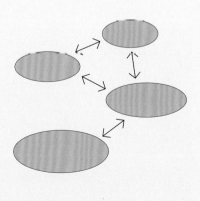

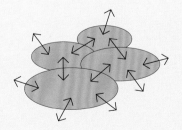

A Performance Art for Public Health

For architects, this will alter practice in profound ways. There will be a move away from the architect-as-global-star, towards a field in which the professional will serve as a facilitator of processes that involve design expertise. This will also enable others – clients, communities and collaborators of all sorts – to participate in and help create the environments they inhabit. With that will come a change in the way we view our field, not as one primarily associated with the visual arts, with an emphasis on the vision of a sole practitioner, but instead as one more closely related to the performing arts, with the architect viewed more like the conductor of a symphony or the director of a play, orchestrating the work of many people to achieve an aesthetic end.

Whereas architects today produce mostly one-off designs for individual clients on particular sites, in the future the profession will also provide designs that people who could never afford the fees of architects or the cost of custom design can download and adjust to their needs. While this will not end architecture's service to fee-paying clients, it will greatly expand the scope of architectural practice. In addition to the current 'medical model' of practice, in which architects provide individual solutions to clients' specific needs, will be the emergence of a 'public-health model', in which professionals will evolve designs appropriate to – and able to be appropriated by – the more than 90 per cent of the human population in need of architectural services but unable to afford them.

The services that architects offer fee-paying clients will change too. Most practitioners now spend a tremendous amount of uncompensated time chasing building projects, which leads to the extraordinary inefficiency and financial insecurity that plague the profession. By 2050, architects will have made a transition along the lines of that made by attorneys in the 20th century, who established long-term relationships with commercial and institutional clients that involve legal services beyond that of going to court. For architects, building design will represent one of a growing number of services they provide, whereby the building itself increasingly marks the beginning of a relationship with a client, not the end, as is often the case now.

The research and programming phase of an architectural project will become much more

important as a result. It will determine whether a client needs a building at all – always the first question every architect should ask – and also reveal myriad other design-related requirements. These may have nothing to do with the building itself, opening up other kinds of services – organisational design, experience design, service design, system design – that will become an ever-growing and ever-more-profitable part of architectural practice.

Such services will eventually lead to mass-customised firms, in which a core group of practitioners will partner with a much wider range of disciplines than typically happens now. Architects may ally with ethnographers to help clients rethink their organisational design, with public-health physicians to help them create a healthier workplace, and with data-visualisation experts to encourage the clients to see new opportunities in the mass of information available to them. By 2050, the most successful firms will have become design strategists, bringing together whatever disciplines clients need to help them achieve their organisational goals.

THE MEDICAL MODEL
OF PRACTICE

The practitioner develops custom solutions for fee-paying clients.

THE PUBLIC HEALTH MODEL
OF PRACTICE

The practitioner develops easily adaptable solutions for millions of people.

THIRD INDUSTRIAL REVOLUTION, 21st century

Digital fabrication has led to an emerging economy of mass customisation, such as this 2011 clothing display system in New York City by Easton+Combs Architects.

44

Architectural Education in the New Economy

This will, in turn, require a change in how we educate architects, as has already begun to happen. Although accreditation standards pose a real barrier to change by enforcing a very traditional, building-centric view of architectural practice, students have begun to vote with their feet, taking courses in a wider range of subjects and even opting for more flexible degree programmes that allow for the hybridising of architecture with other fields. They are recognising the implications of the new economy in which they will work, sometimes better than their professors, many of whom continue to teach a 20th-century version of the discipline. By 2050, building design will have become just one of several tracks – and maybe not the dominant one – in architectural education, much as happened with trial law in legal education.

This will require a change not only in accreditation standards, but also in higher education more broadly. For all of its cutting-edge research and field-shaping theories, higher education remains one of the most conservative and hidebound institutions, perpetuating assumptions not just from the 20th century, but also from centuries before that. The pedagogy in most architecture schools, for example, reflects the mass-production mentality of the old economy, in which students move through a required set of courses and pop out the other end of the educational assembly line with an accredited degree.

While there may be some need for that in the future, the vast majority of the challenges we now face in the world require a much more interdisciplinary and integrative form of education where students and faculty work with colleagues across the university and in the community on the social, economic and environmental dilemmas that continue to confound us. A mass-customisation economy will require a mass-customisation education, and architects should help lead both.

Leadership Opportunities

Indeed, by 2050, leadership could become one of the most recognised and well-rewarded skills that architects have to offer. Too many of today's political leaders remain in power by playing on people's fear of the future, preventing nations from dealing with the enormous challenges facing civilisation, ranging from an exploding human population to persistent income inequalities to global climate change.

Architects lead by helping people imagine futures different from – and ideally better than – what they have now. Every time we design a building, we show people what could be, make concrete plans for how to achieve it, and assuage the fears of those who do not like change and of sceptics who discount anything they have not seen before. Every building project, in other words, builds our leadership skills, and by 2050 humanity will need those skills for problems that extend far beyond those of buildings. Time will tell if we can rise to the occasion. ∞

A mass-production education runs everyone through the same curriculum with standardised results.

A mass-customisation education adapts to the needs of individual students with a diversity of hybrid outcomes.

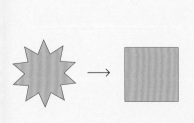

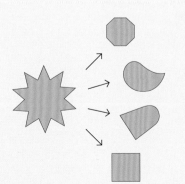

3D PRINTED ARCHITECTURE, 2015

This full-size six-storey tower was 3D printed from construction waste in the Suzhou Industrial Park, Jiangsu Province, China.

Philip Nobel

After Archi

SHoP, Sectional facade study: 3D print.

SHoP, Skin study: 3D print.

SHoP, Structure study: 3D print.

tects

SHoP, Canopy study: 3D print.

A Vision of the Near Future from SHoP

Architectural author and Editorial Director of SHoP Architects **Philip Nobel** evokes a vision of what it will be like to be an architect in 2050, when 'architect' has become an archaic term and building types, such as 'tower' and 'bridge', have become misnomers. This is a world in which architects just 'build', as rich datasets trigger robots to construct 'with the flick of a wrist', and political differences between urban powers have been set aside for the sake of 'civic contraction' so that conjoined cities might persist with the aim of long-term survival.

In the half-sleep of morning, it came to her. Something wasn't right. The same something that had presented itself for a week now, in the time between the slow brightening of daylight-spoofing screens and the gentle storm of mattress pneumatics. A new day. And always now, it was there. Trouble approaching. An inelegance in the scripts, the code of structure and skin.

The question would almost be in reach, and the answer, spinning there in her mind like an antique hologram, blurred where it should be sharp.

Or maybe it was just a dream.

In any case, as the light values balanced and the panes of the bedroom window snapped from milky soft to clear, it was gone.

Every morning: wake, wonder, bathe, dress. Braid her daughter's hair.

'Mom.' A question coming.

'Yes, dear.' Twist. Tuck.

'Why did you decide to become an architect?'

That archaic term. Discovered at bedtime in a 50-year-old picture book. A termite shocks his family when he wants to build with, not eat, his wood.

Charming. That story. Books. Making buildings out of trees.

'I'm not an architect, darling.' Grand figures doling out helpings of Modern Revival glass and steel (as if that made any sense now), sweeping around clients' old-fashioned great rooms in their trendy Frank Lloyd Wright capes. Not at all.

But children are suckers for romance.

'Mom.' Insistent. 'You *are* an architect.'

'No, love.' The braid complete, a final twist. 'I only build.'

A Practice Well Underway

Tower was a misnomer. Bridge, too. But no matter how many times the ministers of two nations corrected the record, the citizens of Brazzaville and Kinshasa would know the construction only as the Tower Bridge. Building for five years now, from the first excavator descents into the red earth beneath Gombe, and still no one would call it the Expedited Transcongo Infrastructure Corridor, despite its tidy French acronym, CITÉ.

Old habits die hard. That was clear to anyone looking at the twinned municipalities facing each other across the slow, wide river. Mile after square mile of sprawl, still, the populations not yet fully reabsorbed into a stable centre, as science and simple prudence mandated, a practice already well underway East and West. Over a decade had passed since the governments of the two Congos had reached an accord, passed their respective laws, drawn the joint urban boundary, begun to charge density fees – 'incentives' – on the farthest flung residents in each domain. Some had come inside quickly, enthusiastically, seeing, as the rhetoric of politicians and NGO consultants told, that it was only through 'civic contraction' – the shorter, cleaner travels closer-knit living would allow; the gentler footprint on the dwindling land; even the improved economic possibilities of what the academics liked to call 'creative proximity' – that the two enormous, conjoined cities might thrive for anything like a 'long term'.

Speeches were made. Pop songs echoed the lessons in a dozen languages. The hated taxes were levied. And the first citizens returned.

Those early resettlers had built joyous camps in the central squares, been welcomed by those already living within the Line – a collective correction, a movement of bodies and minds. And an example mostly followed in the breach. Nature had already begun to consume the plazas and boulevards the returnees left behind. But still their neighbours dallied.

The CITÉ was the answer. The talk of Central Africa and the world. Satellite hyperlapses of the construction became viral darlings in every feed, those same pop songs the pulsing soundtracks. What appeared to grow there, in the few minutes of those videos, was a great rack spanning the Congo River, polygonal CleanCrete trusses situationally deforming to accommodate each gamed-out site condition and load, the network that would bear electric tram routes; car-free, community-gardened side roads; wind, solar and passive hydropower installations; rooftop parklands; schools; hospitals; light and ultralight industry; spacious squares for gathering, celebration, commerce; and enough new housing to shelter every last hinterlands straggler.

It was already a source of enormous pride: 'Take the Tower Bridge to the Future!' ran the refrain of one hit song; 'Live the Good Life in the CITÉ!' urged official adverts on the construction fences. But a suite of international compacts, signed in fearful haste decades before, was coming due. Other incentives, these levied on nations, would soon show cruel teeth.

Faced with a terrible question – how might we persist? – two governments had settled their differences. They had acted. Funds were secured – far fewer than expected from abroad after the massive project itself began to move local economies in a virtuous circle. Now that construction was nearly complete. Primary, secondary and tertiary structures standing over the river. Helical probes trailing below, transferring the water's movement up to accelerating turbines. Markets open. Tramways operational. Residential modules in place. Nothing remained but the enclosing skins, now being laid over all.

The authorities might meet their deadlines. The people might come.

And yet – something was wrong.

A Chance of Uninspiring

That was as plain after breakfast as at waking. As pressing in her garden as in bed. The question spinning there, just out of reach. Perhaps if she were to go there. Old habits. For years she had still visited the site, only a mile from her flat in Ouenzé through ever-more-crowded streets – visited even though the information flowed everywhere the same. At the now nearly outdated virtual reality control booths, from the compact holo-generator in her hand.

Her daughter off to school. The rustle and grind of bundled hair, the motion of the braiding, felt still in her fingertips. The insistent question refusing to take shape. An intuition of trouble.

Power on.

The briefest pause as the device recognised her, purred into life – *Good morning, Nathalie. Work suite?* – and was instantly lost beneath its own projected glows. A nod, and the carefree models from the night before were swept away. A distant clatter.

Now the familiar ghost of the virtual CITÉ, the Tower Bridge, her work. No more complex than the ray-traced pastel forms of her daughter's evening play – spires and pointed arches, a castle for a queen – and no less real. Only resting on richer datasets, more deeply interconnected, and much more likely to be made physical with the flick of a wrist, a pinch of a thumb and forefinger, a closing fist on the grand project coming into being across town.

The bots had made progress since she had last checked in, moments before her troubled sleep. Not good progress, not surprising, only exactly what was expected from the scripts. Skinbots, as these recently deployed units were known, each a dual-mode sinterer: solar by day, conical lenses focusing the equatorial rays, and sipping from batteries at night for normal printing. The slight difference in output between the two methods of fabrication left subtle stripes across the façade – a touch of *wabi sabi* that always made her smile.

The backstory did, too: so human. The sintering tech was the child of an outlandish idea, floated by a writer back in the teens. In 'The Man Who Sold the Moon' (2014),[1] the activist, sci-fi writer Cory Doctorow had imagined self-powered printers rocketed up to roam our cosmic near-neighbour, building there for building's sake. This short story made the rounds, inspired dreaming, tinkering, collaboration, research. A few prototypes were eventually let loose on the Burning Man playa. And finally, when it seemed possible enough, the venture capitalists jumped in. Production, then. Competition. A lawsuit or three. And here we were: 900 semi-autonomous solar-powered sinter-printer robots crawling the trusses of Africa's most ambitious climate-adaptive megastructure.

Climb. Stitch. Weave.

Sometimes, looking down at the activity in the palm of her hand, pinching in for a better view, she would see one of the skinbots flash the tag for Open Gap. Glaziers would follow then, to fill it, already called by their brother bot's code, coming alone or in a swarm to stretch out a sheet of glass or blow a bubble of plastic – locally sourced, of course; except for the rare-earth elements used in the sensor arrays of the CITÉ's internal analytics, all its materials were repurposed from the two cities' waste streams. The cost of transportation, the carbon cost, otherwise, would be more than any rent or subsidy could recoup.

'The slag', everyone called the mixed upcyclables in the streams. With irony, a nod to primitive steel.

Spin. Form. Climb. Extrude.

Climb.

SHoP, Structure study: 3D print.

SHoP, Structure study: laser-cut acrylic.

Stitch.

Weave.

SHoP, Woven pattern cladding study: 3D print.

SHoP, Canopy study, 3D print.

As the day wore on, as they gradually logged in, Nathalie could see the avatars of the other builders. Each tagged to a particular zone of duty. Each probably luxuriating at home, as she was, coffee in hand. Each likely more at peace with what they saw, oversaw, being built by their coded rules.

Better sleepers, she guessed, her colleagues. Many were from elsewhere – transient jobbers, larking expats – some already eager to leave for work on the Next Big Thing. They didn't sweat the small stuff. Kept their eyes on the clock. They never let the glitches get them down.

A glitch. Yes. She could feel it – trouble coming. But where? A parting motion with two hands brought her deeper into the model, revealed rushing layers of backbone data. Power flows. In-process failure tests. Rolling completion projections. And the wind-adjusted schedules of the sailing barges that brought the slag to the site in an unending minuet.

In then past Operations to the picture show of the PR feeds. A stream of best-outcome renderings there, captioned with automated bullet points: how the final result might appear, and what that might mean, projected forward from any given state of the construction.

Current forecast: fair, with a chance of uninspiring.

Deeper now, to Management chatter, Administrative paper pushing, busy regions of HR punctuated by encrypted wellbeing data flowing in from employees' wearables. And underpinning everything, at the deepest place of all, the tens-of-thousands-a-second push of credits into the system from what was itself but another dynamic model: the ledgers of First Transfederal. A node in another living structure, enormous, but one to which she had no key.

Bend. Cut. Climb.

Variable-cost subroutines activated. Reports sent. Receipts filed, approved.

Open Gap. Fill. Merge Planes.

It was rare that the bots required input of any kind – only, at the insistence of distant and conservative insurers, human monitoring. Frankly, Nathalie found, it could be a bit dull. She had begun taking side-work of a much more intimate kind – a gallery in a century-old shipping container, a garage redone for new arrivals. She'd even picked up a saw the other day, just to feel the bite of its teeth against bamboo ply. It felt good. To make decisions on the fly. To design.

The design of the CITÉ, if it was design – the instruction set – was a series of parameters arrived at via the mined knowledge and eventual consensus of hundreds of specialists, generalists and applied data engineers (ADEs) – among them one Nathalie Adoula. They had come together to contribute interlinked rules about aperture density in response to solar load, capacity of reclamation channels, expected microgravity anomalies that might minutely reshape the transformation of the slag. The economics cut everything so close to the bone; there was no room for overbuilding.

But it still had to have a look, and look right. An algorithm based on the form factors of traditional local handicrafts was proposed, and quickly rejected (international backers the rumoured cause) in favour of a risk-free global mean. Now net-crawling code, some of it not quite legal – penetrating fashionable servers, lurking in unposted queues – performed a wicked series of inductions, fed into the model in real time, to ensure that, relative to every other job running versions of the same scripts, or any new Great Work published, or simply to universal human taste as understood by universalising human science, the CITÉ, when complete, would be *au courant*.

Climb. Stitch. Weave.

Nathalie watched her swarm of bots.

Open Gap. Fill.

And she saw in the finished surfaces – something wrong. Quick toggle to the data stream of her daughter's class. A blast of text – 'mom!!! stop!!!! you promised!!' – followed by a retro angry-face emoji and, for a flash, far-side camera thumbed on then off, a scowling nine-year-old, braids flying as she shook her head in mute protest.

'Sorry, dear. Hugs and kisses. I'll be out when you get home after violin.'

The bots coming together, scattering, returning. The surface growing, following up the outside of the structure. Droid armies shifting laterally to the next bay. Her charges were approaching from both sides an inside corner, a kink in the body of the whole introduced years earlier, one of many but the first that would see skin. The re-entrant angle was the perfect sum of structural, mechanical and micro-environmental pressures, checked against the latest spatial psychology reports. The model thought a bend there, almost picturesque, would lure residents. Keep them.

And it might. But – her dread at waking, the almost-question almost answered – something was just … off. Something in the way the skins were behaving, closing in from either side.

Something ….

Something she could fix.

But not here.

A Big Ask

It was always a shock to see the CITÉ itself after studying it for days or weeks in holographic model. Not because it was different, but so similar; that tech had come a long way since her first visit to a science museum. Still, standing at the river's edge, looking across at the span of the Tower Bridge, there were a few things to discover. Reflections up off the water on the underside. The passing shadow of clouds on the flanks. Birds circling the highest towers, then bats. It was late afternoon when she walked to the site, away around to the far side, an extra mile along the fenced edge, to where her own bots crawled. Instant tropical night came as she studied them. They moved now in the white light of the moon, red safety blinkers on their backs.

The model didn't waste its bandwidth with such things. But people did. Always. Still.

Maybe the tech would get there. Close the gap between automation and intellect. Science and romance. Left brain and right.

The infernal gap. Her troubled sleep.

She fished the holo-generator from a pocket, fired it up. Status verified in the airless model and the cooling night. The crease there, the bend in the flank – that was the problem. She could do her own running calculations of collective taste. The corner would need resolution – and whether it did or didn't, truly, it would get it. That was the current style, *au courant*. She guessed her bots would throw a half-round there, an engaged column to turn the inside corner. Perhaps a touch of fluting, for the material savings. Classicism had come roaring back, as it often does, and she'd seen similar details recently on the Consolidator in Detroit.

She closed her eyes to the structures before her, modelled and real. Imagined the flows of data. Intuited the site pressures and constraints. Felt her dread as information.

No. That wouldn't do, a column. It wouldn't solve the problem.

She spun her model back up, checked the probabilities, the projected solutions for that spot. There it was: windows. A run of them right up the crease – 89 per cent likelihood pro.

A glitch. Somehow it had escaped clash detection. The bots might not know what to do. Or – it was possible, still in this bright future; it happened – they would just make a hash of everything. Bungle the geometries in a frantic search for logic. Fill the corner with this and that. Situationally appropriate, maybe, viewed from afar. But nothing that would make the Transcongo proud.

Nathalie felt the urge before it became rational—moved her fingers, her whole hand through the model before more responsible selves might check her motions.

Local forms had been suggested, rejected. There would be more than a trace of that history in the data engines; a nonstarter, the system primed to return 'Request denied'. But, she felt again the gathered threads of her daughter's hair. Twist. Tuck. A simple motion, a series of haptic commands. Bots from each plane jumping across to the next, continuous output there to trail a sheet. Over. Under. Loose enough, it would let in light. Open Gap – glaziers descending then from their rooftop hides to fill the staggered ogives between three crossing strands.

Deeper in the data now, to verify her hunch. Waste Stream State. Materials Pricing. Yes: at that minute, but perhaps not in five or three, the composition of the incoming slag was leaning silica-rich. Seven per cent above running mean. Cure accelerated in the cooling night. Margin enough. For now, just now, it would be cheaper to glaze than to blow plastic. And glass would be more beautiful there when it caught the light.

A glance at the real thing: robots blinking red under the rising moon, closing in.

Back to the model. A grabbing fist and that whole corner pulled off, dropped in sidebar. Design mode.

Twist. Tuck. Twist. Tuck. Run Fill. Repeat.

Repeat to Limit.

'Analyse,' she whispered, only feeling it was right, not taking the time to see. 'Propose typical for condition.'

And the queries went out.

To the Materials Warden's server. To the mainframe of the Keeper of the Clock. To PR renderers and talking-point simulators. To psychology lab databases. To distant, conservative insurers. To the stolen tastes of the style police. To government ministers. To the banks.

One second, two …

It was a big ask. Time enough to wonder if it were too big.

Three seconds …

A hint of change out of the corner of her eye. The bots on the building, the real ones, pausing, downloading a new script, assuming a new formation.

Four seconds – latency! – and her sidebar moved back over the main model, merged there, flashed green under a scrolling report:

Mid-Process Adaptation #1618/J. Analysis follows
Structural: on
Operational: on
Material: on. Efficiency pro-rated to norm:
+5%. Record filed
Temporal: on. Rolling: +3%. Record filed
Formal subroutines … no objection
Propagate: yes
Request approved
Solution output to grid
Process commenced

She turned away from the model, then gazed out across the slow river to the Tower Bridge. A dance of red lights, a dance of robots in the night. She watched them work, but only for a moment. She already knew how it would look. And it was time to get home. ∆

Note
1. Cory Doctorow, 'The Man Who Sold the Moon', in Ed Finn and Kathryn Cramer (eds), *Hieroglyph: Stories and Visions for a Better Future,* William Morrow (New York), 2014.

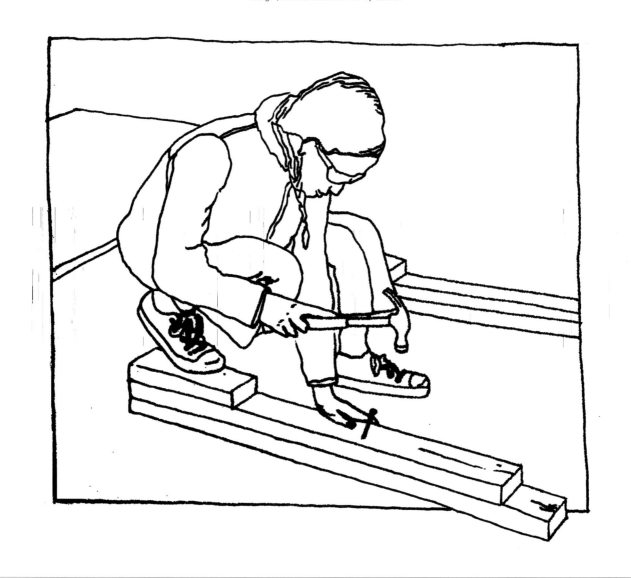

Her, With the Hammer

A Mother's Letter to Her Daughter

Emily Pilloton

Trained as an architect, **Emily Pilloton** is the founder of Project H, a non-profit that runs a design-build high-school programme in Califormia. Here, through her fictional protagonist Agustina, she imagines a future of female self-build self-reliance.

May 15, 2050

To my daughter Frida

You would be 12 years old today. I keep writing you these letters, delivering them to your bedroom as if you will come home from school this afternoon, sit down to do your homework, find my letters and smile. You've been gone for six years, gone for as long as you were here. Today I start a new adventure and I wish you were here to share it.

I have decided to become a homemaker. No, not one those women from a century ago. I'm building a new house. Out on our land, outside of the city which is too gray and loud and fast. I'm making a new home, for me, and for your memory. Remember when you were in kindergarten and I taught you how to use a chop saw? Your teacher thought I was crazy. Your father too. I remember myself at 12, the age you would be today, learning how to weld and build and change a flat tyre while everyone else was falling in love with robots and lasers; 36 years ago. I was so lucky to have those experiences in school, because girls like me were not supposed to be wearing a hard hat over our pigtails. No matter how far we came, equity was subjective, opportunity limited, especially for little brown girls like us.

I built a bookshelf for my teacher once, after school while the boys were playing soccer outside. The principal asked her where she got it, and she told him: 'Agustina built it.' He asked, 'Who?' and she told him, 'Her, with the hammer,' winking at me from across the room.

I am still that woman, that mother, the one who fixes what is broken and makes things beautifully by hand. These days, Frida, if you were here, it would not be a question of girls and boys. Things are more equal now. But that day not so long ago when we used the chop saw, when you were five, we were outcasts. Now it is hand versus machine. Of what button we can press, not what our hands can mould and shape.

And so I'm building this house by hand, for you. I'll use the wood from the land and that old chisel your grandmother gave me. I'll mix the concrete by hand and handpick each cedar shingle. I will design a space for us, filled with light and love, a room for you and your books and your blocks. It's so important to make things, Frida. It is through our hands that we carry on our story. How I'll tell yours. And since you aren't here with your hammer to build it with me, I will build it for you. ∞

Always, Your ever-loving mother,
Agustina

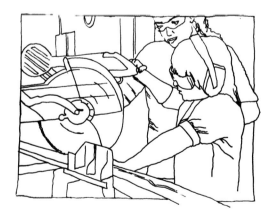

I taught you how to use the chop saw as a very young girl.

It's Not Where You're From,

Polygraphic
illustration

September 2014

Mark Watts

It's Where You're At

Mayors are taking bold action to build and run their cities in ways that are sustainable: good for the environment, while increasing the health, wellbeing and economic opportunities of urban citizens.

Looking back, 2015 was a pivotal year. I was 12 months into my role as Executive Director of the C40 Cities Climate Leadership Group (C40) – a network of representatives from megacities across the globe acting to reduce greenhouse gas emissions.[1] Although I thought it was the best job in the world, I never expected that now, 35 years later, I would only just be retiring! But as city leaders came to play such a central role in creating our new low-carbon world, it was impossible to leave.

What Happened

It was not a massive technological breakthrough that changed things – most of the solutions we needed were already being practised somewhere (as the examples below illustrate). Rather, it was that city leaders worked together so that what had been hundreds of isolated examples of urban sustainability became common everywhere.

Climate change and sustainability expert **Mark Watts** imagines what it might be like to look back from the year 2050. What might the view be from his position as Executive Director of the C40 Cities Climate Leadership Group? What crucial political moves and actions might be required from global megacities if they are to address climate change and make the ultimate shift to a low-carbon world?

Today everyone knows that the Global Parliament of Mayors is more important than the United Nations in terms of solving big global problems. But in 2015 people saw the UN's Paris Climate Talks between national leaders as the last chance to constrain emissions within 'safe' levels.

Well, there was a deal in Paris; but had the commitments made by nation states been the only outcome, the world would now have experienced a devastating and irreversible change to our climate. Instead, after C40 mayors had marched alongside 1 million, mostly young, people demanding radical action in Paris, the mayors got together to launch a major programme of urban renewal that set the coordinates for a low-carbon world. Leading on from this, seven years later there was a second, much stronger, climate treaty, helped by the fact that some of the most prominent C40 leaders had become prime ministers and presidents.

Sustainable Cities

Thankfully cities today look nothing like the grey, wet, dystopian view of our urban future in the science fiction of my youth. In fact, so green are most cities that it is quite hard to spot the boundary between city and rural hinterland (Janine Benyus, see pp 120–21, would be pleased!).

True, this rise in urban greenery was necessary to protect against rising temperatures and increasingly dangerous weather. Ho Chi Minh is a case in point, where the mangrove swamps are even more prevalent now than before the big development take-off in the 1990s, thanks to the natural flood-protection properties they provide.

The need to grow urban food was also a stimulus as rural crop yields declined in many countries. Ever since the Milan Expo of 2015, farming has been steadily creeping back into cities. There is nothing new about urban agriculture, of course; and even in the year 2000, one billion city farmers produced about

15 per cent of the world's food. Indeed, in Addis Ababa, the model of smallholdings adjacent to many homes has remained in place throughout the intervening half century. But in places like Milan, Tokyo and New York, hydroponics is queen and much of our food is grown indoors in farms that stretch to the sky.

You Can Only Manage What You Can Measure

There is another reason why our cities today are so green, and it started with the mantra of former C40 Chairperson and New York Mayor Mike Bloomberg: that you can only manage what you can measure.

It seems ridiculous today, but the prevailing view in 20th-century economics was that all value was created by human activity and measured by the price that commodities could fetch in an open market. Thus it was somewhat unusual when in 2014 the Mayor of Melbourne asked his staff to conduct a survey of the value of the city's natural resources. It took a few years for this new science to bear fruit, but today pretty much every mayor is obliged to publish an annual statement of natural capital.

Average surface
temperature
distribution

Rotterdam

1998

Since 1984, Rotterdam has mapped the city's urban heat island, which poses a serious threat to the health and wellbeing of citizens. Adaptive measures such as tree planting and cool roofs are just some of the solutions cities worldwide are implementing to become more resilient to the impacts of climate change.

293 <
296
299
302
305
308
311 >

A Unique Combination of Universal Elements

More or less everyone lucky enough to live in one of the world's great metropolises will claim that their city is like no other. But with city mayors now working together so closely, today it's more helpful to say that each city is a unique combination of universal elements.

In fact, from an urban planner's point of view, the basic design of the biggest cities looks quite familiar everywhere. This is not a bad thing, and C40 can take some credit here, because after the publication of the New Climate Economy report by the Global Commission on the Economy and Climate in 2014 and its second city-focused report in 2016, we really picked up on its 'three Cs' formula for delivering sustainable cities – compact, connected and coordinated.

At the heart of the 'three Cs' formula is the notion that successful cities have dense rather than sprawling urban forms. Copenhagen was the model, with its 'five-finger' spatial development model that only permitted major new developments near to major public transport nodes.

Indeed, transport – or 'connectedness' – focuses on ensuring city-dwellers have a high degree of mobility based on a hierarchy of walking, cycling, public transport, plus a few private electric and bio-fuelled cars. In the 20th century, urban planners had come to believe that cities should be designed for cars. Garages – homes for cars – came to be almost as big as human dwellings. Vast areas of city centres were taken up with places called 'car parks' for vehicles to rest during the day while their owners were at work. Space for noisy, polluting vehicles took priority even along beautiful coastlines and

amidst architectural wonders (although a brave Mayor of Rome pedestrianised the area around the Colosseum as early as 2014). What was really weird was that most people, at least in the wealthier countries, thought they needed to own at least one car, despite the fact that on average they used them for less than an hour a day. Now, of course, everyone is in a car club and even companies like BMW sell mobility services, rather than actual vehicles.

My old mentor, Ken Livingstone – the former Mayor of London, was one of the first to usher in a shift away from car use by introducing a 'congestion charge' on motor vehicles, alongside a massive programme of investment in buses, cycling and the metro. By the mid-2020s, pretty much every major city had done the same. But the most dramatic example of a change in 'connectedness' was in Rio. I remember my first meeting with the pioneering Mayor of Rio, Eduardo Paes, back in 2013. He was about to become my boss as Chair of the C40 and he arrived for our appointment covered in dust from having just pushed the button to blow up a six-lane highway to make way for a massive expansion in Bus Rapid Transit (BRT). Three years later, as Rio welcomed the world to enjoy the 2016 Olympics, 60 per cent of the trips were being made by public transport, cycling and walking – a threefold increase from when Mayor Paes took office. Now the number is closer to 90 per cent.

PARK(ing) Day

San Francisco and Oakland, California

Rotterdam, The Netherlands

Brooklyn, New York

2008-12

above, below and opposite top: Converting parking spaces into urban 'parklets', the PARK(ing) Day campaign has been celebrated across the globe since 2005. Artists, designers and citizens collaborate with cities to raise public awareness about the need for more urban open space and alternative modes of transportation.

It is hard now to remember the levels of congestion we had to put up with when private vehicle use proliferated, or how noisy it was when motor vehicles were fuelled by petrol. Shenzhen was, and still is, the centre of electric vehicle manufacturing. But it was Oslo that became the first to have its whole public transport fleet powered by renewable energy. Personally, I'm still cycling, and everywhere seems to have 'gone Dutch', following Amsterdam's example in providing high-quality cycling infrastructure across the city to give almost everyone the confidence to cycle where they choose.

Coordinated Cities

Perhaps the most important part of the 'three Cs' formula for sustainable cities has proved to be the focus on 'coordination'. There has been a big emphasis on understanding the city as a system in which, for example, decisions about water or waste management also impact on transport services or building design. But more than that, mayors have discovered that they deliver best for their own citizens when they learn and copy from successful policies in other cities. That is what the C40 is all about; and more than anything else, it has been cities' ability to cooperate with each other that has elevated mayors above prime ministers and presidents as leaders in tackling climate change.

Self-Reliant Cities

Another important issue is cities' autonomy in terms of power supply. Cities used to depend on power from national grids. Today most big cities are self-reliant for at least a third of their electricity needs, following the example of Scandinavian cities like Stockholm and Copenhagen. Public support has been achieved by giving citizens affected by renewable energy installations a financial stake in the company.

The creation of a Cities Climate Fund was also an essential step, providing grants to develop new low-carbon projects and direct loans to city governments (bypassing slower-moving national governments) to finance green infrastructure investment.

C40 mayors

Climate Week

New York

2014

Solidarity among mayors to tackle climate change is a driving force behind international co-operation on this issue. At the UN Climate Summit in 2014, C40 mayors from cities including Rio de Janeiro, Paris, Johannesburg and Seoul showed unity and ambition to help countries meet and exceed their climate targets.

Lower Carbon Means More Liveable

Of course there have been big problems over the last 35 years, many of which remain. Although we managed to avoid runaway climate change, with average global temperatures pushing 2 degrees above pre-industrial levels, the impacts have still been very severe. Each year I join millions of others on 1 August in remembering the thousands who died in the 2030 water riots.

Yet overall, I think most people would agree that the world is actually a much better place in 2050. As one of my favourite rock stars from the old days, Ian Brown, once drawled: 'It's not where you're from, it's where you're at.' It has turned out that cities can deliver prosperity without it necessarily engendering ever-increasing exploitation of the world's non-renewable resources; and, while we all consume less, on average people are happier.

Oh, and Benjamin Barber was right – mayors do now rule the world![2]

Notes
1. The author wishes to acknowledge the C40 and its member cities for providing most of the examples cited in this article, along with Jonathon Porritt, whose book *The World We Made* (Phaidon (London), 2013) has been the inspiration for what a vision of 2050 could look like.
2. See Benjamin Barber, *If Mayors Ruled the World: Dysfunctional Nations, Rising Cities*, Yale University Press (New Haven, CT), 2013.

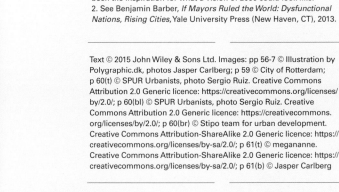

The Street As Platform

Dan Hill

'Museum of Future Government Services',
UAE Prime Minister's Office with
Tellart and Future Cities Catapult,
Government Summit, Dubai, 2015

The Museum of Future Government Services, a vision of how advanced technologies can
transform government services for the better, was a three-day immersive experience featured
at the Government Summit in Dubai. Here, responsive facades provide hyper-localised air
conditioning by tracking movement and emitting cooling vapour only where it is needed.

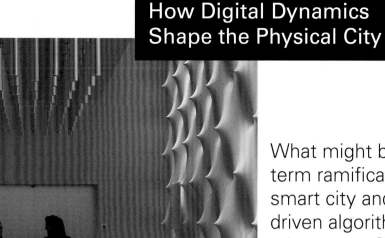

Personal clouds of cooling follow people as they walk under this canopy, more effectively conditioning an environment.

How Digital Dynamics Shape the Physical City

What might be the long-term ramifications of the smart city and big-data-driven algorithms on physical urban space? Designer and urbanist **Dan Hill**, Executive Director and Chief Design Officer of the UK innovation agency Future Cities Catapult, fast-forwards to 2050, taking the opportunity to imagine the physical reality of 'the street' in an age of eerie silence, drones and lush foliage.

The way the street feels now is increasingly defined by elements that cannot be seen with the naked eye. Data-driven services like Uber and Airbnb, the emerging 'Internet of Things', social media and mobile connectivity, 'big data'-driven algorithms: these are already shaping the urban experience, even if they are difficult to perceive.

A new kind of city is emerging, an algorithmic city. It promises gleaming efficiency, citizen-centred services on demand. Yet the algorithms that produce these conditions – political, economic, cultural – are similarly to parse, and are quite different to those that shaped cities previously. Anthony Townsend notes that 'the tools that have governed the growth of cities – the instructions embodied in master plans, maps, and regulation – have long been considered a matter of public record',[1] before pointing out that this is no longer the case as we drift towards the smart city.

Perhaps by speculatively fast-forwarding some of these conditions to 2050 we might better understand and articulate what is beginning to happen in today's cities?

At a Crossroads
Imagine film of a normal street in 2050. A relatively busy crossroads at 9am taken from a vantage point above, looking down at an angle as if from a CCTV camera or James Stewart's apartment in Alfred Hitchcock's *Rear Window* (1954). We can see several buildings, a few vehicles, and quite a few people, and pavements dotted with street furniture. To the right, a train station. To the left, a row of apartment buildings.

Freeze the frame and scrub the film backwards and forwards a little, observing the physical activity on the street. But what can't we see? What defines the street in 2050?

The first impression is not visual, but aural.

It is quiet. The only prominent noise is that of a few nanocellulose tyres on the street; every now and then, a soft, somehow distanced 'swish', as if they are throwing their voice. Drones buzzing around overhead are also quiet in the main, their ultra-light bodies bobbing and weaving in the gentle breeze. Birds can be heard clearly, as can wisps of conversations. An old coffee machine sputters and hisses. Music drifts from apartment windows.

Much of the street is woven with lush foliage – clumps of grasses, small trees, creepers curving around fabricated mesh forms. These winding pathways are designed to handle storm water as well as to breathe, and have thin rivulets of irrigation cut into them. Thickets of trees shade the street along one side. On the other, a slender curving structure floats above head height, its struts and lattice strewn with subtropical vines and flowers. It provides further shelter, protecting cyclists and walkers from the sometimes intense sun; on a hot day, which is most days around here in 2050, it emits a delicate, fine mist of cooling vapours that follows people as they pass through it.

Full-scale prototypes of autonomous vehicles, illustrating the many different configurations of driverless cars that may become available.

Although most movement, other than walking, seems to be via a wildly diverse set of bicycles, occasionally flocks of 'drivers' swoop through the streets, curving gracefully around the greenery and any other obstacles in their path. Over time, these largely autonomous vehicles have carved a broad sweep through the foliage; or rather, the greenery has slowly encroached on what was once road space, in a symbiotic relationship with the drivers. There is no real definition between street and kerb, and building and flora. Forms ease out of one into the other. Streets are broad canyons of activity, as rich with biodiversity as they are with diversity of people, work and play.

There are perhaps three or four drivers every five minutes, each of varying shapes and sizes depending on function. Some carry one or two people, others nine or ten. Some drivers carry goods, others are mobile workplaces, bars, medivans or civic service touchpoints. There is no parking as far as the eye can see – drivers slide in, pause briefly to pick up, drop off or interact in some other way, and then exit the stage left or right, heading for their next appointment.

The city's civic intelligence system – dubbed 'Lestrade' – is based on an atom-thick membrane of nanocellulose derivative, woven with microscopic smart dust in a form of low-resolution circuitry applied to many surfaces of buildings or infrastructure, some foliage, most drivers and so on. Stretched taut over the city's fabric, it is essentially invisible, but it is there, constantly sensing its state. Bridges and tunnels are anxious hypochondriacs, looking for cracks in their structure before they occur. Mercantile streets are counting footfall to predict likely commercial activity, with property values fluctuating every few hundredths of a second accordingly. Every breath of air, every footstep, every shift in

temperature as the sun creeps across the stone is generating data for the city's intelligence, helping refine the current set of 'predictions'. Older buildings have the plasticky membrane spray-painted onto them, in places of likely stress – either physical or social.

Racks of 'slivers', paper-thin curving films of flexible grapheme display, can be found fanning out from the slender lighting poles that sprout alongside the wattle trees, although the odd flash of reflected sunlight reveals that a few semi-translucent slivers can also be seen discarded on the various benches and tables that punctuate the street's gardens.

A sharp-dressed man wearing glasses picks one up and it flares into life. It pulls down his ID via fingerprint and rapidly unfurls a series of updates, largely image based, with the occasional blare of audio coned for his ears only. His predictions rattle up the screen with a slight flick of the wrist. He mutters something under his breath to the sliver. The sliver, using its creaking 5G connectivity, borrows a few processor cycles from the lighting pole he is passing before switching its attention to a park bench as it, too, is passed by the increasingly broad strides of the man. Finally the sliver hops onto a meatier access point baked into responsive kerbside.

The kerb, which is usually flush to the street, raises a few bumpy nodules as it recognises the man is visually impaired. The temples of the man's glasses are threaded with small sensors, and gently graze his cheekbones, a bone-conducting speaker conjuring a 3D soundscape about his immediate environment, enabling him to navigate it with some ease, particularly when combined with the haptic feedback from the subtly raised street surface underfoot.

The man feels for a nearby lighting pole, and leaves the sliver in the communal rack. The sliver's shape memory rolls itself up into a tube, its glow dissipating as it transfers any excess power into the lamp's grid. The man steps out into the road, the traffic flowing around him like a river around a rock.

Moving past him across the road, a woman with an implant over one eye is gracefully carving shapes with her hands in front of her, manipulating unseen information elsewhere.

On an oversized sliver hanging across the street, hoisted on thin, almost invisible cables, a countdown to today's 'extreme': 'Prediction: 8 hours and 14 minutes until tonight's extreme. Flavour: subtropical cyclone. Intensity: category 1.' The slender rectangular screens sitting underneath the few remaining street signs flicker into life, their jittery physical pixels shuffling rapidly before settling on a single message denoting that City Algorithm No 33 – 'Blue Dahlia' – is in effect, as virtually everyone knows.

A group of people starts to form by the roadside below, tapping wearables, moving closer to each other. They are edging towards a spot where a small constellation of pinprick

By 2030, some autonomous vehicles may effectively be workplaces on wheels.

lights indicates a 'predicted social driver stop' will shortly appear. The shuffling phalanx becomes a moving queue, a concentration of datapoints. Across the street, a smaller group of around three or four people is also trying to summon a 'social driver'. They simply do not have the numbers, though. A stout man in the first group shouts across for them to 'Give it up and join us'. Three people from the second group trot across the road. The group must have achieved critical mass, as a social driver (size = M) soon appears around the corner, its side panel popping up and over with a hydraulic sigh. The social driver sets off, calculating the optimum route for the various destinations of the passengers. The errant member of the second group decides to wait a bit longer for a 'personal driver', and heads off to the coffee shop for a swift espresso.

The entrance to this design futures exhibit, speculating as to 2030, featured augmented reality datapoints floating over the street scene.

A flock of drivers suddenly appear from nowhere and swarm towards the station. Some of them display the yellow livery of the city's public transit agency, and others have the iridescent nanocellulose shells of a private business called Drosje. They move with what most still consider a slightly eerie jittery gait, their intelligence constantly shuffling them around in relation to each other, a little like Venetian gondoliers jockeying back and forth on a rolling grey tide. They near-silently glide towards the station's curtain wall, a volley of whistles, inaudible to humans, indicating 'handshakes' and 'exchanges' between each other.

Their immediate physical presence and movement may appear unpredictable, yet the drivers have been generated in response to a prediction of the likely traveller needs on the incoming train – based on previous patterns for this train at this time, combined with the personal histories of each passenger on board this particular journey, combined with a few 'active requests' at the last minute. Drosje vehicles seem to be here in greater numbers, their Norwegian intelligences perhaps a little more tuned to this situation. Still, the average accuracy of this prediction is approaching three 9s, meaning that neither drivers nor passengers have to wait; the 'fit' is virtually exact and the 'idle' is essentially zero. The station broadcasts to other drivers around a 5-kilometre (3-mile) radius that this train has already been taken care of, just as the train slides to a standstill.

The passengers' wearables ping the drivers, negotiating a price (the destination is predicted, for the moment – it can be calibrated en-route) in a few milliseconds, and all drivers swiftly wriggle their way back through the station's verdant landscape.

In the distance, behind the station, a skeletal set of struts sketches out a line for a few hundred metres, festooned with subtropical flowers and, occasionally, tomato vines and climbing beanstalks. It is the abandoned ruins of Crossrail 3, a major transport infrastructure project cancelled due to advances in predictive transport. Like an algae-filled canal, it marks a shift in mode and the end of an era; the end, in fact, of constructing new transport infrastructure to deal with increased demand in favour of optimising movement on existing streets via prediction and autonomy. Few new buildings or infrastructure have been constructed during the last 16 years.

Overhead, a drone shuttles over to an apartment block in the near distance, its onboard sensors preventing it being buffeted by micro-therms and unpredictable gusts. It hugs the building's rippling edge as it begins to descend, cleaning the facade's faceted photovoltaic cells.

Further overhead, in the inky thermosphere in fact, various satellites serve this crossroads with real-time mapping. Tiny scratches of light embedded in the road below shimmer to convey their presence as they pass above. There is a near-constant twinkling to the road's rubbery fabric.

There is a happy, excited chatter in a tarp- and tree-covered playground to the left of the street, as a class of schoolchildren crowd around a set of slivers pushed together to make an impromptu larger display. They are watching the remote launch of a nano-sat for their collaborative project with a school elsewhere, having parent-sourced a few hundred euros to cover the cost.

A young woman enters from the left, glancing occasionally at the road markings, and the odd drone buzzing around overhead. A bead of sweat runs down her brow, a snail trail over her hi-definition make-up. The make-up is a form of dazzle camouflage, applied via an inkjet 20 minutes previously. It conceals her true identity from the city's intelligence, throwing it off her scent with subtle occlusions and extensions sketched across and around her eyebrows and cheekbones. As she weaves through the thin crowds, her digital wake is composed of a series of purposeful errors. This pattern ripples destructively through the predictions, building exponentially just as traffic waves used to cause traffic jams. Each step constructs a form of data junkspace. She allows herself a smile at the small pockets of 'failure demand' she is depositing around the city's infrastructures.

To the left, a cleaning robot scuttles in and out of view. It is servicing a row of refactored buildings, just as they receive a new prediction about their immediate energy needs.

Set in 2030, municipal workers maintain streets alongside municipal robots.

Exoskeletons may augment the abilities of municipal workers doing manual street repairs.

Note
1. Anthony Townsend, 'Legibility and Interpretability in Predictive Models (of Cities)', Medium. com, 19 December 2014: https://medium.com/@anthonymobile/legibility-and-interpretability-in-predictive-models-of-cities-687680b39274.

A maintenance robot as municipal worker.

To the left, a cleaning robot scuttles in and out of view. It is servicing a row of refactored buildings, just as they receive a new prediction about their immediate energy needs. They rapidly handshake in order to shuttle energy back and forth, in and around the block. Two buildings have a brief argument over surplus solar energy, which each is trying to trade with the other, several times per second. Neither wishes to be idle.

Several of the houses have been rebuilt with nanocellulose exteriors. These are slight, with street noise barely an issue, yet tough enough to withstand the extremes. Most of the buildings here date from the 19th and 20th centuries, but have been refactored to comply with carbon strictures. As sunlight falls across a glassy 1960s block, the algae in its facade blooms slowly to cool the building's interior.

At the end of the row, a mycelium drone, its cargo bay empty, settles gently onto the top of the buildings' shared compost heap as the aircraft's batteries fade. The bacterial cellulose and proteins coating the drone's rough-edged structure begin to slowly decompose. Within a few minutes, little will be left. The compost's knot of rotting root vegetables is enriched by the drone's bodywork-cum-protein-shake, something Lestrade duly notes and conveys …

And Pause

As algorithms responding to real-time data begin to replace the 'dark matter' of building codes, ordinances and plans, and models based around snapshots, our cities will be shaped, operated and experienced in entirely new ways.

While there are clearly immense benefits to a city taking advantage of predictive and responsive code, we must ensure that the dynamics of those approaches, as complex as they are, will be understood, debated and shaped not least by the disciplines that drove previous eras of city making. Sketching this street corner is not about predicting 2050; it is about articulating the entirely new form of urban design that is being prototyped around us right here, right now. ⌂

A Century of Ecological Innovation

As humanity faces its greatest disruption to date – climate change – placing the planet and its long-term survival in jeopardy, visionary designer **Mitchell Joachim** of Terreform ONE incites optimism. Rather than being defined by disruption, he predicts that the 21st century with be characterised by innovation, which 'promises to solve the global challenges we face'.

We are called to be architects of the future, not its victims.
— Richard Buckminster Fuller, in Steven L Sieden, *A Fuller View: Buckminster Fuller's Vision of Hope and Abundance for All*, 2012, p 101[1]

Innovation distinguishes between a leader and a follower.
— Steve Jobs, in Carmine Gallo, *The Innovation Secrets of Steve Jobs*, 2010, p 7[2]

Looking forward to a future that shines is not a platitude; it is an absolute imperative. All designers, by their very nature, are empowered to speculate about the near future. In fact it is the point. The act of invention is the governing rule of remarkable design. To grasp the imperceptible and make it visible is the most powerful instrument a human can wield.

Terreform ONE

Fab Tree Hab

Massachusetts Institute of Technology (MIT)

Cambridge, Massachusetts

2001–

A living graft prefab structure.

Tomorrow is an unshakable discourse. Everything must draw from its past, connect the dots and venture onward with farsightedness. Design in its best wide-ranging procedures formulates the stratagem for tomorrow. Without a shadow of a doubt, the art of imagination is a limitless attribute of humankind. Cases in point: Walt Disney, Elon Musk, Norman Bel Geddes – society is still enthralled by the futures they promoted. If imagination is used for positive intentions and checked against deleterious effects, its ascendancy is humbling. The 21st-century future faces an immense disruption, that of climate breakdown, and depends on design to innovate our path forward.

What will be the predominant narrative for the 21st century? Each era has a philosophy of advancement and decline, of blossoming and withering, of expansion and devastation, otherwise known as an idea of progress. Every age also has a concept about the previous and the existing, of what elapsed and what persisted, a view of temporality and notion of what is defined as historically significant.

Philosophies of historical narratives used to be paranormal: the heavenly governed time; the finger of divinity, an extraordinary sagacity, lay beneath the plunge of every species. If the existing differed from the historical, it was habitually wicked: mystical concepts of the past leaned towards degeneration, a descent from refinement, the loss of a deity's support, dishonesty. The 18th century encompassed a sense of expansive progress; the 19th century had evolution; the 20th century had development and then modernisation. The terminology that defines this century is debatably disruption, but more accurately it is innovation. Innovation promises to solve the global challenges we face and to reorient humanity.

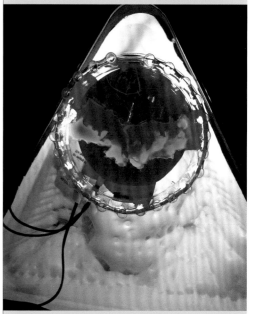

Terreform ONE

Bio City Map of 11 Billion: World Population in 2110

2014

100 per cent connected mega-urban regions: the world as one social ecology.

The existing urban population is expressed in bioluminescent E-coli in green. Projected future population is expressed in red.

Why innovation and not disruption? Parts of the hyper-mediated landscape of our age have defined this period as the era of disruption, which, despite its promise, is crude. It is a notion created on a weighty nervousness about economic cessation, panic of worldwide climate Armageddon, and the difficult correlation of evidence. Many individuals suffer from anxiety that connects stock market cycles, pandemics or climate to everyday occurrences. Disruption is too often perceived as mischievous or even damaging. Yet, as a society we must seek innovation and not the negative symptoms of disruption. Innovation is the healthier narrative of today and it has many variants. What tomorrow will look like critically depends on current innovations.

Innovation is like painting a watercolour in a stream. It is difficult to express, especially against vast relentlessly changing systems such as climatalogical episodes. Climate change and associated environmental problems, although disruptive, are best solved through stimulating acts of invention. Copious innovative designers and architects make bold claims about environmental recovery. Unfortunately, others capitulate to economic limits at the expense of the environment. Starchitects are affordable for less than 1 per cent of the population, and most of them pay only lip service to ecosystem basics. The other 99 per cent of the population favour designs for a salubrious society.

We have had this impression before, that we could be at a crossroads, that we are learning devastating data, that there is a grassroots rebellion for change. The litany of events that led up to this after the second half of the 20th century is familiar enough to us. In 1946, one year after the bomb was dropped at Hiroshima, John Hersey's shocking account in his book of the same name portrayed the vast and continued destruction of a city and almost everything in the surrounding environment.[3] Atomic desolation was the first time humankind realised that it is entirely within our power to end nature. Soon after, accounts of humans distressing the earth became more commonplace. The early battle calls have been cited over and over.

In 1953 the *New York Times* published its first article on the budding subject of global warming.[4] Rachel Carson's 1962 bestseller *Silent Spring* etched the issue of environmental degradation, especially with widely used dichlorodiphenyltrichloroethane (DDT), into the world mindset.[5] In 1970, gatherings around the world

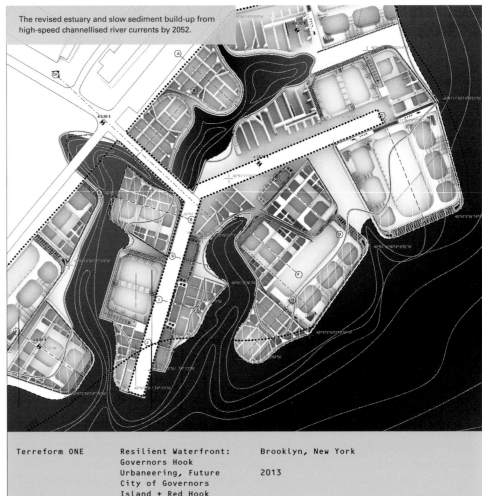

The revised estuary and slow sediment build-up from high-speed channelised river currents by 2052.

Terreform ONE   Resilient Waterfront: Brooklyn, New York
                   Governors Hook
                   Urbaneering, Future   2013
                   City of Governors
                   Island + Red Hook

Recycled military vessels help to create the soft water's edge to facilitate stormwater absorption and climate adaptation.

celebrated the first Earth Day – with over a million celebrants in New York's Central Park alone.[6] And in 1989 Bill McKibben's thoughtful and urgent call to action in *The End of Nature* inspired a generation of environmental activists.[7] Today, a veritable cottage industry of manuscripts exists around the topic of sustainability, from Betsy Kolbert's

The Sixth Extinction (2014)[8] to Timothy Morton's *Hyperobjects: Philosophy and Ecology after the End of the World* (2013)[9] to Edward Mazria's '2030 Challenge' initiative to reduce fossil fuels and develop an adaptive, resilient built environment.[10] People have been raising awareness and participating in public debate on environmental matters since 1946. How much longer do we need to proclaim the planet is in jeopardy?

As stated earlier, we need to move forward, and now is the tipping point. Since 1958, the Keeling Curve has charted the atmospheric carbon dioxide atop Hawaii's Mauna Loa volcano.[11] Scientific consensus has set the safety threshold at 350 parts per million (ppm);[12] by June 2014 it had risen to almost 405, exceeding the treacherous threshold of 400 ppm. In 2014 the UN released another sobering report on climate dynamics, decades after the Rio Summit and Kyoto protocols.[13] It bitterly declared that most prior carbon-emissions reduction obligations placed on the leading developed nations remain ineffective. It also announced that numerous developing countries have increased carbon output. The time has come for immediate action.

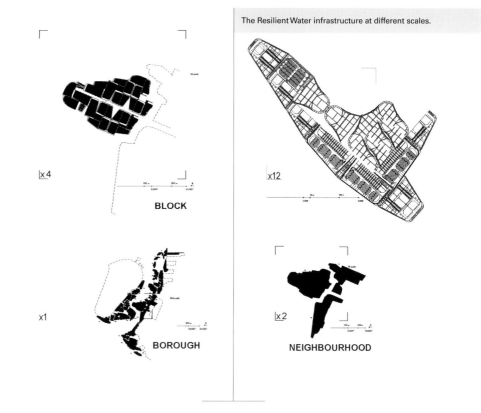

The Resilient Water infrastructure at different scales.

x4 BLOCK

x12

x1 BOROUGH

x2 NEIGHBOURHOOD

People have been raising awareness and participating in public debate on environmental matters since 1946. How much longer do we need to proclaim the planet is in jeopardy?

Masterplan of Governors Hook: a new combined neighbourhood that includes Red Hook in Brooklyn and Governors Island in Manhattan.

From 1991 to 2011, 97 per cent of all peer-reviewed published research on climate change affirmed that humans have triggered the precipitating events.[14] Major world scientific institutions concur.[15] Yet only 66 per cent of the media supports the concept of anthropogenic global warming and, unfortunately, 55 per cent of the American public believes there is scientific disagreement.[16] The good news is that there is time to close the gap, but not much. Nowadays, even drastic emissions reductions will take decades to reverse the damage. We are locked in for substantial added global warming from the greenhouse gases already emitted. We must face our failures head on. It is our duty to correct the course. Humanity bent this futile path and therefore humanity can reverse it.

Terreform ONE

Gen2Seat: Genetic Generation Seat

2012–

A full-scale synthetic biological chair grown from a biopolymer of acetobacter, chitin and mycelium.

From 1991 to 2011, 97 per cent of all peer-reviewed published research on climate change affirmed that humans have triggered the precipitating events.

Terreform ONE

In Vitro Meat Habitat

Genspace, New York

2008

A victimless shelter 3D-printed from extruded pig cells to form real organic dwellings.

We will need to act in accordance with the UN as we already face the sixth mass extinction event ever identified in geological time. The epoch of the Anthropocene, which started with the Industrial Revolution in the late 18th century, will come to an end.[17] China is thrusting forward with a colossal scheme to transfer 250 million rural inhabitants into freshly minted cities by 2025.[18] Mega-planning cities from scratch, or rather warehousing, is a forceful action that could set off an upsurge of growth or burden the republic with difficulties for decades. How this is implicated into a world perspective of resource consumption is up to the world of design. Design can reveal these impacts to the public. Designers have the capacity and authority to convince us that change is coming and we can do better.

The projects featured here, by the Terreform ONE (Open Network Ecology) design group, defy apocalyptic climate-change scenarios, and are predicated on the near future. They range from transportation and architecture to global plans, and all are a profound response to contemporary urban design and quotidian city dwelling. Our century is about innovation, and these projects intentionally push forward the upper limits of what is possible. If we cannot think and experiment in vast terms, we cannot solve vast problems. ⌂

Terreform ONE

Soft Car: Lambs

2003–

Soft inflatable air-quilt vehicle using low-pressure soy-based pillows for the body.

Notes
1. Steven L Sieden, *A Fuller View: Buckminster Fuller's Vision of Hope and Abundance for All,* Divine Arts (Richmond, CA), 2012, p 101.
2. Carmine Gallo, *The Innovation Secrets of Steve Jobs,* McGraw-Hill Education, (Columbus, OH), 2010, p 7.
3. John Hersey, *Hiroshima,* Alfred A Knopf (New York), 1946.
4. 'How Industry May Change Climate', *New York Times,* 24 May 1953.
5. Rachel Carson, *Silent Spring,* Houghton Mifflin (Boston, MA), 1962.
6. Congress took the day off, and the morning show 'Today' devoted 10 hours of coverage to it. For a summary of the events, see Nicholas Lemann, 'When the Earth Moved: What Happened to the Environmental Movement?', *New Yorker,* 15 April 2013: www.newyorker.com/magazine/2013/04/15/when-the-earth-moved.
7. Bill McKibben, *The End of Nature,* Random House (New York), 2006.
8. Betsy Kolbert, *The Sixth Extinction,* Henry Holt and Co (New York), 2014.
9. Timothy Morton, *Hyperobjects: Philosophy and Ecology after the End of the World,* University of Minnesota Press (Minneapolis, MN), 2013.
10. http://architecture2030.org/.
11. The data was first plotted by Charles David Keeling, and is maintained by the Scripps Institution of Oceanography at the University of California San Diego. See Jeff Tollefson, 'Uncertain Future for Iconic "Keeling Curve" CO_2 Measurements', *Nature,* 20 November 2013.
12. James Hansen et al, 'Target Atmospheric CO_2: Where Should Humanity Aim?', *Open Atmospheric Science Journal,* 2, 2008, pp 217–31.
13. Intergovernmental Panel on Climate Change (IPCC), *Fifth Assessment Report,* United Nations, 2014.
14. John Cook et al, 'Quantifying the Consensus on Anthropogenic Global Warming in the Scientific Literature', *Environmental Research Letters,* 8 (2), May 2013.
15. Naomi Oreskes, 'The Scientific Consensus on Climate Change', Science, 306 (5702), 3 December 2004, p 1686.
16. *Ibid.*
17. Marion Glaser, 'Human-Nature Interactions in the Anthropocene: Potentials of Social-Ecological Systems Analysis', Routledge (Oxford), 2012.
18. Ian Johnson, 'China's Great Uprooting: Moving 250 Million into Cities', *New York Times,* 15 June 2013: www.nytimes.com/2013/06/16/world/asia/chinas-great-uprooting-moving-250-million-into-cities.html?pagewanted=all.

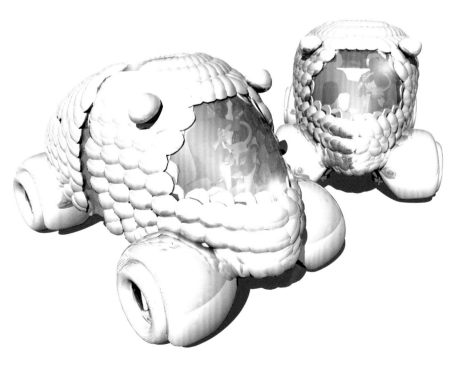

Nataly Gattegno and Jason Kelly Johnson

Future Cities Lab,
Hydramax,
San Francisco,
California, 2011

Hydramax port
machines extending
from the city out into
the bay.

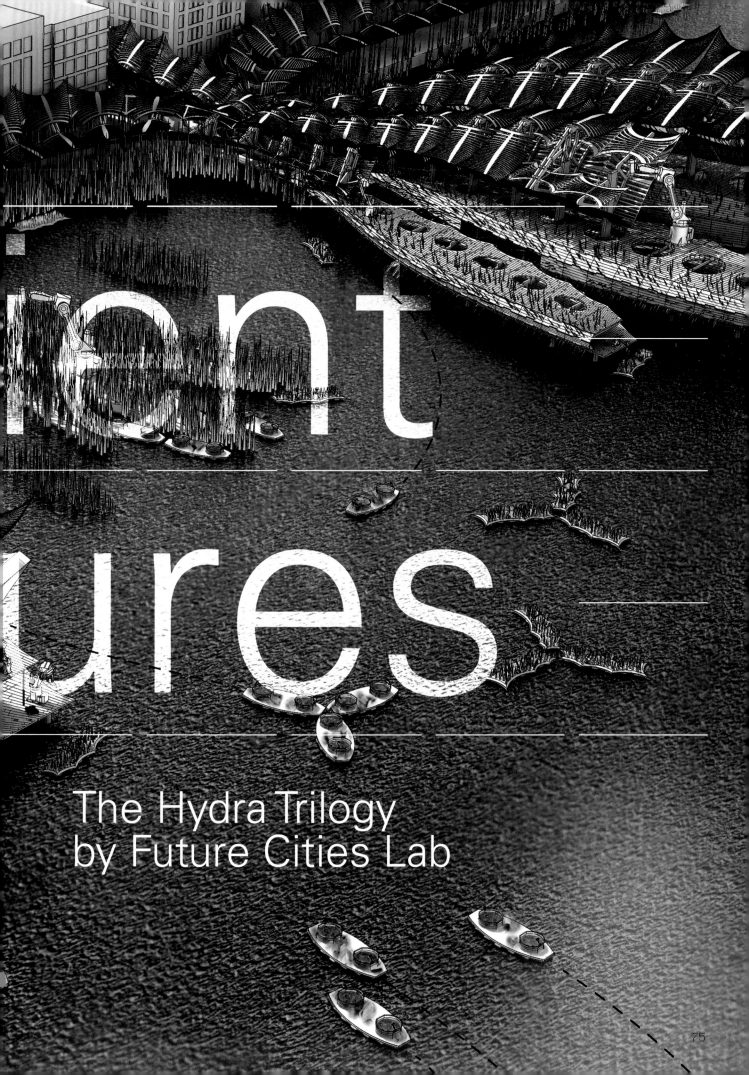

The Hydra Trilogy
by Future Cities Lab

Nataly Gattegno and Jason Kelly Johnson, the founding principals of San Francisco-based Future Cities Lab, conjure up a vision of the parched, forever thirsty California of 2050, beset by water scarcity and the extinction of its natural species.

Future Cities Lab,
Hydraspan, San
Francisco, California,
2013

Hydraspan layers multiple systems and ecologies: water collection, water filtration and fog harvesting coupled with food production, human occupation and transportation.

The Golden Gate City has morphed into a Hydramax urbanscape, vacillating between growth and decline; every tectonic feature becomes an opportunity for moisture capture, whether the Bay Bridge or roofscapes, facades or the streets themselves.

The Hydraspan colony: a highly productive environment that synthetically recombines production and living with infrastructure.

She trudged west through the Embarcadero marshes, beneath the span of the abandoned Bay Bridge, to a high point out front of the clock tower. In her bag were specimens she needed to deposit in the Theater of Lost Species. If she couldn't find it among the aqueous ruins of the city's former edge, she would have to release the little three-eyed creatures back into the bay. In the distance, suspended from the bridge trusses, the immense, glowing fog-catching ribbons of the Hydraspan colony gently swayed with the wind. Fog was rolling in this evening and the catenary ribbons were descending quickly to harvest fresh water. This was her home.

After the drought and ensuing conflicts, much of California was rendered barren. To the south, the urban sprawl that occupied the former desert regions of the state was largely abandoned. Hydraspan and other water-scavenging enclaves along the coast began to take form. These days every surface of San Francisco – its roofscapes, facades, streets – was enlisted to capture moisture. The Bay Bridge was now a large-scale water catchment and storage machine; fog ribbons harvested water, filtering and storing it in large sacks suspended from the trusses of the rusting bridge. Robotic skypods descended into the bay as fishing and transportation platforms. Among the gigantic trusses, a new live-work colony, greenhouse and parkscape inhabited what used to be traffic-congested roadways. The colony's globular forms pulsed in a daily ritual of growth and decay.

Future Cities Lab,
Hydramax,
San Francisco,
California, 2011

Hydramax fog-catching feathers reaching into the sky to harvest water for the embedded hydroponic and aquaponic farms.

Public spaces of Hydramax are woven with technology, food production, infrastructure and transportation.

She observed the fog bank forming over Yerba Buena Island and quickened her step as she waded back through the Hydramax marshlands. At the end of the Folsom Street pier, which split to form the open-air markets of the Hydramax port machines, she paused to take in the scene: flotillas laden with the day's catch were coming in for the night and the market bustled with evening shoppers. The glistening fog feathers above slowly reached towards the sky; after a day of harvesting solar energy they ascended to their fog-catching position for the evening. The water collected from the atmosphere was being used to supply nutrients to the array of hydroponic gardens and massive fish farms. Machines continuously learned to optimise urban farming technologies to supply the city's food needs. Robotic farmers tended to the gardens and fish,

harvesting food for the markets embedded in the Hydramax, and transporting surplus across the bay to distant enclaves.

She caught a glimpse of the iridescent green robot tucked away under the bridge, glowing as it searched for new specimens. She had heard that the Theater of Lost Species had recently documented a series of creatures rumoured extinct after the sea-level rise. She did not want to miss the performance. She followed its tracks, and came upon a small crowd of spectators peering into the attenuated portals of the theatre. Looking in she discovered awe-inspiring images of our very recent past, a virtual menagerie of species recently gone extinct; the glowing, beautiful, magnificent victims of our own evolution. The theatre gave her a glimpse into this archive of lost species it had captured, documented and

archived in its travels, to which she could gratefully now contribute.

The performance was breathtaking, albeit tinged with melancholy. She left the theatre as it scanned her offering and began her trek back to the glowing city. It was a transformed city, a reconstituted city, a patchwork of old structures from her childhood and new, synthetic layers pulsing with life. The city had become a sentient machine, glorious, autonomous and alive. ◬

Future Cities Lab, Theater of Lost Species, San Francisco, California, 2012

The Theater of Lost Species searching for new specimens to archive.

The city had become a sentient machine, glorious, autonomous and alive.

Looking through large glowing viewing cones one sees creatures near extinction swarming in a virtual fish bowl.

Interdependence

A Manifesto for Our Urban Future, Together

Lisa Gansky

Social media and online collaboration has enabled a greater level of connectedness, heralding a new era of belonging or global community through person-to-person collectivity. Entrepreneur and innovation adviser **Lisa Gansky**, Chief Instigator of Mesh Labs and the Instigator Collective, anticipates the impact of enhanced technology-enabled interdependence on the future life of our cities.

Luz Train Station,
São Paulo, Brazil,
February 2014

Connection drives change. Human connection, accelerated by technological innovation, fuels the urban landscape and the interlinked lifestyle – today and tomorrow.

Saída / Exit

When we try to pick out anything by itself, we find it hitched to everything else in the Universe.
— John Muir, *My First Summer in the Sierra*, 1911[1]

We experience the perplexing tension between brazen self-sufficiency and our irrefutable connectedness as we meander through our daily routines. We are already living the prototype of our urban future. Looking ahead today's trends signal a more connected, agile and collaborative global community. Cities remain the seed bed for innovation, and innovation can only emerge from an open and optimistic perspective of our future. Technology plus people-powered communities and platforms invite unprecedented advances, coupled with a sense of belonging. While the last century saw the birth of the global corporation, we are now witnessing the nascent power of the person-to-person collective. We are deeply connected and must develop together to flourish as a global society.

City as Platform

For the first time in history, the majority of the world's people live in cities.[2] Cities, as never before, shape our experience and our future. They are a palpable platform for crowdsourcing our lives; they are our most pervasive, sustained example of humankind's capacity to make, adapt and self-organise. Urban citizens are connected as never before, through mobile phones, meet-ups, pop-ups, co-working spaces, collaborative housing, shared transit services and globally driven local crises. Already we are swept up in Internet-driven change through the social media-fuelled Arab Spring and the Occupy phenomenon. Born in, and spreading quickly from, the dense hotbed of cities, they highlight the most essential competence

of the next 30 years: our ability to rapidly, agilely and continuously self-organise, responsively re-designing our communities, companies and networks.

Technology-Enabled Interdependence

As physical proximity meets the digital footprints of our search queries, transit pathways, mobile chats and financial transactions, our ever-more connected activity is continuously illuminated. Data transforms the invisible into vibrant networks. For example, personal mobility data gleaned from 'wearables' reveals routes to run, cycle and walk; pulsing maps of activity constantly emerge from pooled data across various types of sensors. Imagine the hyper-dynamic maps and insights flowing as these data combine with connected vehicles, buildings and living systems. Such insights spur responsive urban planning, zoning and incentives to improve daily life.

While data reveals information previously concealed, our peer-to-peer interactions divulge who has what, needs what, when and where. The sharing economy has tapped into temporal 'waste', converting excess capacity to value and unearthing massive utility from what we already have. As a global community we have so much, but much of what we have we are not using to its capacity, including talent, goods and services. Existing online platforms already address some of society's urgent needs, especially for urban dwellers. With platforms like BlaBlaCar, Neighborly, Huertos Compartidos, Couchsurfing, FabLab and Open Explorer we are already developing a new kind of social operating system, enabling us to solve local issues while opening a global dialogue. Tighter connections shift our social operating system from an orientation of the individual to the power of peers in collaboration.

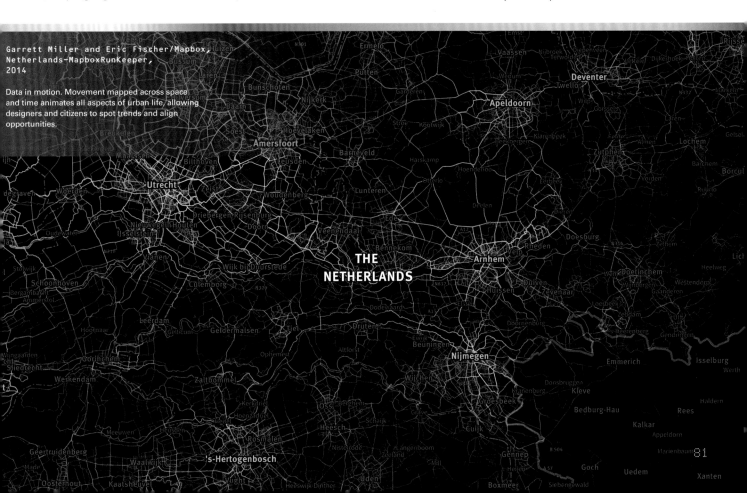

Garrett Miller and Eric Fischer/Mapbox, Netherlands–MapboxRunKeeper, 2014

Data in motion. Movement mapped across space and time animates all aspects of urban life, allowing designers and citizens to spot trends and align opportunities.

Urban Hives

Cities, like living organisms, take shape as a perpetual process. No place is more exemplary of the temporal, flexible mesh of humanity than our cities. The combination of technology plus empowered people fuels accelerated open learning, sharing and innovation across geographies and sectors. Mutable pop-up experiences are a permanent way of life, while connected buildings and infrastructure are made robust and supple. Once networked, these assets can be effectively designed, utilised and maintained. Whole cities can adeptly reorganise in real time, anticipating demand and shaping local code accordingly.

In the years to come, as fluidity and adaptability become the norm, urban dwellers will turn to their neighbourhood to leverage local connections, physical assets and the strengths of their peers. Taking cues from some of nature's most resilient citizens like honey bees, urban self-organising communities emphasise the social intersections or touch points within buildings, neighbourhoods and local ecosystems. As sharing economy thinking pervades our collective understanding of life, work, home and play, networks of people increasingly look to each other to create community-based confidence, wealth and resilience.

By 2020, expect to see leading cities explore the idea of Community-as-a-Service (CaaS), a concept that borrows inspiration from the software industry's Software-as-a-Service or SaaS business models. This 'as needed, access based' approach invites local groups to create decentralised peer-to-peer production and distribution of energy, water, food, recycling and communications services. Self-contained, hyper-local systems will prove to be far more resilient and less expensive than last century's 'centralised' utilities. These CaaS models will be refined and shared rapidly, allowing each new service to adapt to local customs and environment. Large-scale corporations will adapt by cultivating early signals of success, propagating leading models and innovators.

The Grid of Personal Power

As the carbon economy wanes and the demand for new solutions grows, energy production and distribution will spark from the power of sharing and creative collaboration. As each contributor generates power, communities will go beyond zero energy to build surplus. A new grid will form, each contributor representing a point on an open, shared power network. Experiments in personal solar-generation services are already expanding through the efforts of companies like GRID Alternatives and Solar Mosaic. Personal pods, walking, streets, buildings, parks and food are just some of the means we will use to gather the power for our cities.

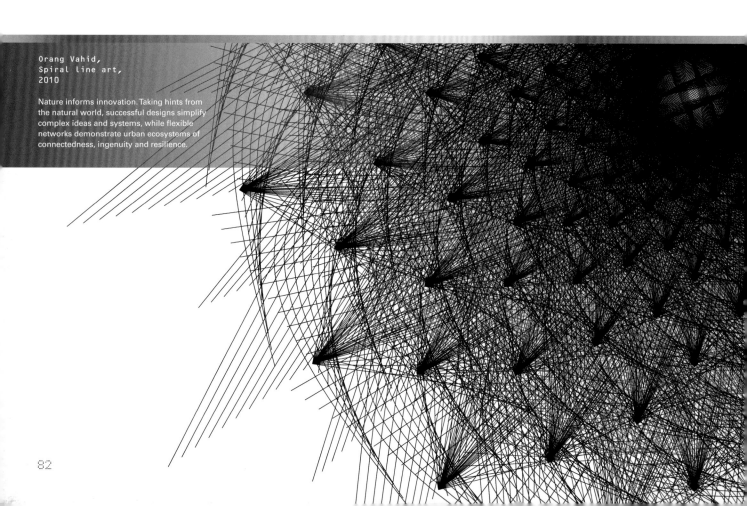

Orang Vahid,
Spiral line art,
2010

Nature informs innovation. Taking hints from the natural world, successful designs simplify complex ideas and systems, while flexible networks demonstrate urban ecosystems of connectedness, ingenuity and resilience.

Inspiration for solutions will continue to be drawn from nature. Taking the Fermat spiral[3] as a muse, designers and engineers might partner to create a new approach to solar energy. When mimicked by a series of mirrors, the spiral would create a highly efficient and spectacularly beautiful solar array. Resembling nature's own sunflowers, these arrays – 'bloom powers', perhaps – could soon grace everything from parks and buildings to homes and streets.

As we each generate our own energy, opportunities to 'bank' surplus come from the peer-to-peer, district-by-district mesh of hyper-local production and distribution. Run as a community-owned service, electricity – followed quickly by food and water – will be in the hands of local networks that generate, secure and deploy it. Centralised utility companies link neighbourhoods and businesses as producers and users of energy, water and other currencies. Those utilities that survive shift to an open-source platform model, connecting networks, sharing best practices and unlocking 'innovation on tap'.

Resilience in Numbers

We humans will show ourselves to be a resilient bunch, redefining our ideas of shelter, food, wellness, work, adventure and community in ways that feed our families and our spirits. The crowd, which today is often experienced as a nuisance by-product of urban living, will be increasingly seen as a mutual safety net. Routinely, the people, communities and ecosystems best at tapping into the power of the crowd will rise above those who stubbornly remain unto themselves. This results in a clear bias towards banding together to solve our most profound challenges. Trust is the currency that fuels agile urban societies. Interactions become fluid through a global open currency – perhaps 'bitseeds', which will grow in value as community ecosystems develop and deepen.

The power of networks of people – shaped by demand and opportunity, propelled by open innovation – is the foundation for our urban societies. The momentum for urban innovation is the force generated by the push and pull between and amongst us as we look towards the future together. The more we embrace the tension between self-reliance and interdependence, the better future we will create together for our cities, and for each other. ᴆ

Notes
1. John Muir, *My First Summer in the Sierra*, Houghton Mifflin (Boston, MA), 1911, p 87.
2. According to the United Nations, 54 per cent of the world's population lived in cities by 2014, and by 2050 we are likely to see 66 per cent of the world's population become urban dwellers. The urban population is set to grow from just under 4 billion in 2014 to 6 billion by 2045, including those living in more than 40 'mega-cities', with more than 10 million residents each. Source: www.un.org/en/development/desa/news/population/world-urbanization-prospects-2014.html.
3. www.encyclopediaofmath.org/index.php/Fermat_spiral.

Junior school children exercising, Beijing, China, 2007

Diminishing the distance between us. Striking the right balance between self-reliance and interdependence is how we will forge our urban future together.

One of the most powerful women in Swedish business, **Karin Lepasoon** has been widely recognised for her ethical values. Previously Executive Vice President of international construction and project development company Skanska, she is now Director of Communications, ESG and HR

Karin Lepasoon

Healthy Humane Buildings

at Nordic Capital. Here she looks back from 2050 and describes how wellbeing has become central to the design of the built environment, underwritten by new technology and solid bottom-line numbers.

Running on empty:
Transbay Terminal
building construction,
San Francisco,
California,
2014

This barrel was seen during a site visit to the Transbay Terminal building. It is a representation of the industry that became an empty shell of itself by focusing on the wrong aspects of value.

It is strange now to consider just how much we focused outward in the past. We believed in migration to the moon or Mars as the only way forward for our civilisation. I am thankful our actual approach was far more down to earth; a focus inward on the cosmos of our buildings and their influence on the health of our bodies. Here, in 2050, we put human wellbeing at the heart of our building designs, and the result has been nothing short of remarkable.

We knew as far back as the early 2000s that a sound indoor climate with fresh air, reasonable thermal comfort, healthy materials and natural light was as vital to our health and productivity as nourishing food and deep sleep are for our bodies. It took us far too long to recognise that creating a resilient society held the key to financial success.

Health-Scanning Technology Starts The Trend

The apps and devices at the heart of this change, introduced at the beginning of the century, monitored our physical status. We had up-to-the-moment reports of our heartbeat, stress levels, blood pressure, and the number of steps we took or stairs we climbed. Devices extrapolated to understanding our emotional state by 2020 and, finally, in the 2030s, understood the holistic picture of wellbeing. This health-scanning technology reminds me of the old-fashioned GPS satellite navigator, except it tells us so much more about the places we want to live, work and travel.

People began steering their work and leisure activities towards environments that positively affected their health. A dreary school that caused distress for its kids saw declining enrolment. Apartment buildings that were uninspiring sat half empty. But an office building, known as healthy through online feedback about non-existent sick days, had waiting lists for tenants. Consumers wanted to hear this kind of news to make informed decisions, and businesses leaned on traditional media to create shows focusing on success stories. The private-sector businesses and NGOs got it

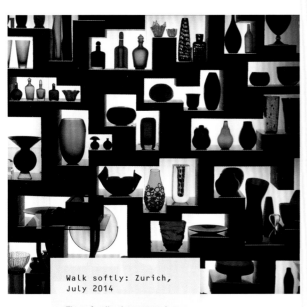

Walk softly: Zurich,
July 2014

These fragile glass vases shot in a gallery in Zurich remind us of the instances of software and hardware artefacts that can now empower the integration of the virtual and physical in a seamless fashion. This object-oriented thinking was a critical enabler to progressing integrated design.

A high GHI increased health, harmony and productivity. It became the only metric that mattered.

The fantastic voyage:
Gardens by the Bay,
Singapore, 2014

The aspirations of so many were
ignored for a long time. This venue
in Singapore was only successful
due to holistic cross-governmental
collaboration focused fully
on citizen wellbeing. It is an
inspirational exemplar.

first, and then builders started to listen closely. It was impressive how quickly they respected and embraced the rating system that grew out of the monitoring. Soon it was the best way to differentiate the companies that valued people's gross happiness index (GHI) and understood the positive impact of this on their financial bottom lines. A high GHI increased health, harmony and productivity. It became the only metric that mattered.

Life-Cycle Costing Embraced

The game changer really was when regulators around the world put in place relevant laws to push using only the lifecycle cost of a building when developing society – taking into account up front all the costs of a building over its entire life instead of separating the construction cost from the operating cost. The public sector, governments and taxpayers had simply grown tired of seeing sub-optimal calculations turn into more expensive operating costs, and people then avoiding the buildings because of their ratings. It did not pencil out anymore.

The lifecycle cost approach evolved to produce ultra-high-performance buildings and delivered ultra-high-performing humans almost as a by-product. This was the beginning of a completely new era with human wellbeing at the core of all decisions, investments and ventures.

Overhead: San Francisco, California, 2014

The recognition that total lifecycle costing was necessary in order to make the transition to sustainable design was often considered blue-sky or even pie-in-the-sky thinking. By the middle of the century the new regulations, recognising human wellbeing as the central issue, introduced the inclusion of holistic parameters including externalities that had been ignored for too many years.

As a consequence, successful employers now ensure that their stores, offices, markets, schools and hospitals enhance people's health. These buildings – with individual temperature control, improved ventilation and natural lighting – can boost productivity by more than 20 per cent. If staff costs amount to 90 per cent of a typical workplace, then even a small increase in productivity gains or reduced absence due to sick leave far outweigh any extra cost in achieving a higher-rated workplace. And not surprisingly, sales increase in higher-rated retail stores and supermarkets with more daylight and improved lighting.

High-Performance Results

Step by step, we made smart decisions to create environments that enhanced our performance at work, how well we learned at school, how we recovered from illness, and even how we slept after a day at work. It was incredibly affirming.

We found out that a 21°C indoor climate makes a perfect learning environment. Students' results improved. Today it is common knowledge that increasing heat by a mere centigrade cuts performance by 3 per cent. Days in hospital are reduced by 8.5 per cent, and use of pain medication by 22 per cent, in hospital rooms with daylight and a view of nature. Hospital design has become an active part of any cure.

I like these examples of doing well by doing good. What used to be a mere feeling of being uncomfortable in an environment ('This room makes me tired ' or 'It is so hard to concentrate here') is now translated into hard facts and figures. What used to be soft values have become solid bottom-line numbers.

We are building smarter. And we are all healthier and so much happier as a result. ⌂

Media

Network

Three Moments From the
Future Post-Manufacturing
Supply Chain

What will be the post-manufacturing future of the industrial heartlands of Southeast Asia? Fiction and non-fiction author **Tim Maughan** teams up with speculative architect and educator **Liam Young** to capture a dystopian vision of desolate dereliction in 2050, in which large-scale mass production has been almost altogether abandoned in favour of small-scale, local 3D printing shops.

Liam Young,
New City:
The City in
the Sea,
2014

Still from the 'New City' series. 'The City in the Sea' imagines the development of a multicultural city, drifting in international waters and built on the foundations of the Pacific Ocean garbage patch. The original animation was developed with an accompanying short story authored by Pat Cadigan.

Here be Dragons

Ningbo is the last stop before Busan, and then after South Korea it's a couple of weeks of isolation until he hits the European shipping lanes. Maybe Surya will get off there for a few hours, head into town and grab some barbecue. A beer or two. Or maybe he won't.

He got off here, at Ningbo, once before. Never again. Maersk's ground agent gave him a lift into the city – to the forest of towers that line the horizon beyond the vast, dead port – and with a concerned tone told him not to stray too far from the central plazas, not to venture into the residential areas, and that he'd pick him up and take him back to the ship in four hours. Surya didn't really get the concern; it hardly seemed dangerous. There was nobody here, the city having emptied itself when all the factories closed, the people – presumably – drifting back to their families and farms in the country. Nothing seemed to be open either, no shops or restaurants. Eventually he had found a tiny place to have dumplings and a beer, before killing time until the agent picked him up walking the empty streets, watching the digital information displays and interactive billboards, and listening to the city talking to itself.

It had unnerved him. Not the isolation, the lack of people – he was used to that on the ship, relished it even – but the ghostliness of the buildings, how they seemed to have become huge, towering monuments to a dead era. It unnerved him how progress had so coldly left them behind, like a graveyard where nobody came to pay their respects anymore. People back in India said there were places like this there too, but he had no plans on going and seeing for himself.

He sips coffee from a mug that looks old enough to have been made in a factory, and absentmindedly stares out of the windows of the ship's bridge, watching the vast bulk carrier's micro-drones inspecting the complex mesh of tanks and pipes, valves and pumps. As he watches they become almost indistinguishable from the dragonflies swarming over the decks, and just as alien. He has no idea what they do, what they see, what they find. They talk straight to the ship, and the ship talks straight to the network, straight to Copenhagen. Nothing talks to him. He's mainly just here for insurance purposes, a lone babysitter employed because of a legal technicality.

The air above the bridge is filled with klaxon sounds, beeping and synthesised Chinese voices, as the last of

They talk straight to the ship, and the ship talks straight to the network, straight to Copenhagen. Nothing talks to him.

the vast cranes backs away from the ship. As tall as one of the abandoned housing blocks, the huge nozzle still dripping with an unknown, freshly refined print medium. The last time Surya was here the port itself was as abandoned as the city towers, but today there's activity within the valleys of shipping containers; construction workers have set up camp, a makeshift township more vibrant than what he saw that time in the city on the horizon. Workers shipped back in to work on the secret construction project just offshore, presumably. The Chinese government isn't saying what it is, but Surya has seen the rumours buzz across the shipping networks when he's logged in to share music files and Bollywood movies. Some say it's a news island, a floating city. A deep-sea rare-earth mining platform. But the most persistent ones claim it's something even bigger: the start of a vast pipeline, a network that will stretch right across the China Sea and out to the oceans beyond, so that they can cut out Maersk and the other middle men completely and just pump that print medium right into the rest of the world's front rooms.

Surya laughs to himself and shakes his head. He guesses that'll be the end of his babysitting job, when the network needs even fewer moving parts. He guesses that'll be his time to be left coldly behind by progress.

and how they're trying to screw the 'little man'. In this scenario Feng is, of course, the little man. He's always the little man.

Sha just wishes Feng would shut the f*** up now, to be honest. It's nearly 1am and he should have gone home an hour ago, leaving him to the nightshift on his own. Plus his being here means he can't get on with his own plans to screw the little man.

Eventually Feng does shut the f*** up, and before he's even got out the front door Sha is tapping his PIN into the workshop entrance and letting it scan his face. Inside he fires up two of the five automobile-sized printers that they use for bigger

Liam Young,
New City:
Bulk Carrier
Megatanker,
2014

Still from the 'New City' series of animated near-future skylines. 'Bulk Carrier Megatanker' is an 'exaggerated present', imagining the evolution of the global shipping industry from an infrastructure for the transportation of outsourced, manufactured objects into a raw materials distributor for locally produced 3D-printed goods. The original animation was developed with an accompanying short story authored by Tim Maughan.

On Demand

Feng is ranting again, his standard screed about media prices. About how the Chinese are screwing everyone. About how he's heard reports (translated: read bullshit rumours on the timelines) that the Chinese government phones up refineries in Mongolia and tells them to stop production for a couple of days just so they can artificially keep prices high. Feng reckons it's all revenge tactics, that Beijing is still angry about losing its manufacturing base to 3D printing shops like his,

jobs, letting them run through their pre-print cycles in a cacophony of servo bursts and low-level humming. Before they settle down he's already plugging a tiny thumb drive into the first one's control panel, scrolling through its touchscreen with impatient finger-flicks, searching for the correct files. He's got pretty much everything on here, from kettles and microwaves to dishwashers and electric car engines. All the top brands. The best DRM-cracked print files the dark-net file-sharing sites have to offer.

'Honey, what's that cardboard tube in the hallway?'

'That's the TV, come and see.'

Tonight he's got two orders to fill; one new bed for his cousin out by Busan's old port, the other a TV for one of his neighbours in the Samsung condo block he just moved into. The bed should be a quick job, but the TV looks fiddly – it's one of those brand new LG models, ultra-HD, 100-inch rollable screen – and the software is estimating a six-hour print time. Plus his customer wants him to print a box too, so that nobody knows it's a knock-off. He laughs. People are so f***ing precious, especially about brands, but they love not having to pay for it.

Sha gets everything running, gets outs of the workshop before the smell of the chemicals burns his nostrils and makes him nauseous. It's going to be tight, time-wise, getting both jobs done before Feng gets back in the morning. Only thing he can do now is cross his fingers and hope there are no jams or glitches, and have a little chat with Feng's accounting and stock control software. Time to cook the books a little so he doesn't notice where his precious overpriced medium has gone. Maybe he can make it look like it's just Beijing screwing the little man again.

Keeping Up Appearances

Duri drops the Samsung Galaxy SX phone onto the kitchen table, and hears it chime softly as it makes contact with the paper-thin Samsung Qi SmartPower charging mat.

'Honey, what's that cardboard tube in the hallway?'

Sang's voice comes back from the lounge, muffled by the low hum of the Samsung AHT24WGMEA/XSG air conditioner.

'That's the TV, come and see.'

'What?'

Liam Young,
New City:
Keeping Up
Appearances,
2014

Stills from the
'New City' series.
'Keeping Up
Appearances' is
an extrapolation
of the observed
conditions in
South Korea
where technology
company
Samsung has
now moved
into residential
property
development.
The original
animation was
developed with
an accompanying
short story
authored by Tim
Maughan.

'It's the packaging the new TV came in. I've just hung it.
Come in here and see.'

Duri pushes open the door to an explosion of pixels
the width of the room; an ultra-high-definition orgy of
thrown paint and 4K rainbow ejaculate soiling pristine
whitespace. White turns to black, paint to fireworks, stars
flicker and become city lights, a forest of pastel-shaded
corporate branded condo-blocks emerging from the night
as the final strains of the orchestral score fade into the air-
con's never-ending drone.

Sang waits until the TV's start-up and calibration routine
has finished before turning to Duri, idiotic childish glee
filling approval-seeking eyes.

'Nice, huh?'

'Yeah. It's great. But why does it say LG on it?'

[beat]

'Because … it's made by LG?'

'Move it. Now.'

Sang looks confused, almost hurt.

'The TV?'

'The packaging first. Get it out of the hallway. Bring it in
here. Now.'

'What? But they're coming to get the recycling tonight.'

'Exactly. Get it in here before anybody sees it.'

Duri curses silently for trusting Sang with such an
important consumer decision, anxiously glancing at the
feed from the hallway's Samsung SND-6011R dome
camera via a Samsung SmartGear 7 Neo wristwatch.

'Christ, who knows who's seen it already … I just hope
nobody from the building standards committee is back
from work yet.'

'Baby …'

'Don't baby me. Are you trying to get us thrown out? Our
lease is up for review in three months and you brought an
LG TV into a Samsung housing block? What the hell will
the neighbours say?' ⌀

Empowering Communities Through Design

Francesca Galeazzi

Francesca Galeazzi is an architectural engineer who leads the sustainability team at Arup Associates in Shanghai. Here she looks back with hindsight from 2050, reflecting on how rapid urbanisation in China, which started in the 1990s, played out over the next half-century. She describes how the initial highly centralised, mass urbanisation programmes gave way to a more local and community-based, participatory approach to decision-making and planning, foreshadowed by some key legislation around land ownership and design for community-based planning models in the early 2010s.

The last harvest:
the former Han Jia
Wan village, Xi'an,
Shaanxi province,
China, 2010

In the 1990s, China embarked on a huge urbanisation programme, moving most of its rural population into new and existing cities. The scale of this urbanisation was unprecedented and represented the largest human migration in the history of our civilisation, involving 700 million people over six decades. Today, in 2050, it has stabilised, with 76 per cent of the Chinese population now living in cities.[1]

The top-down execution that made this incredible achievement possible had initially failed to include communities in the decision-making process. Where the first phase of urbanisation focused on providing infrastructure and hardware, the later stages started to inevitably include social issues such as preservation of cultural identity, liveable cities and community participation.

In this fast-urbanising China, stakeholder consultation was a marginal requirement of the planning process, or was carried out far too late after plans had already been drawn up. Gradually, local governments started to facilitate citizen engagement[2] through more participatory and transparent governance mechanisms.[3] Due to the fast growth of social media and micro-blogging,[4] communities became capable of reaching out for information and organising themselves to exert more influence on matters that affected them directly.

In 2010, Xi'an, the capital of Shaanxi province, was a city of large-scale urbanisation and infrastructure projects. Rural communities that were being swept away to make space for new developments started to literally grow their houses in demand for higher compensation (based mainly on square metres of living space) ahead of their forcible eviction. This type of resistance was possible where communities acted together, sharing information and strategies to increase their resilience. Since then, community consultation has made steady progress, and in many cities the signatures of at least 99 per cent of stakeholders are now required for the approval of new developments and plans.

However, it still took many years of rapid development to fuel GDP growth before things started to change and the forced evictions across China that had made international headlines were phased out.[5] In 2011, after 12 years of debate, a new law was finally passed to improve citizens' land ownership rights and make it more difficult for authorities to displace them.[6] At the same time, architects and urban planners in China, until then slaves of a rigid planning system controlled by land developers, started to question their role in shaping the future of Chinese cities. The extreme case of the Xi'an rural villages had demonstrated that all affected communities need to be involved and represented in the planning process from the outset.

Community planning was particularly important in China. The notion of 'community' had always been the fundamental pillar of Confucian society, as opposed to the more individualistic societal structures of the West. For the Chinese 'feeling good about themselves is likely to be tied to the sense that they are in harmony with the wishes of the groups to which they belong – the clan, the village, the family – and are meeting the group's expectations'.[7] However, the rapid urbanisation and rush to embrace Western lifestyles contributed to the transformation of the communal character of the Chinese city and to the demise of traditional social models, as low-rise interconnected and vibrant neighbourhoods were replaced with large clusters of high-rise apartments that alienate the individual[8] and displace traditional community structures.

Within this context, in 2010 Arup Associates in Shanghai began to look for alternative models to help China solve its numerous urbanisation issues, by proposing clusters of smaller interconnected and resilient communities that share amenities, community centres and key facilities. There was no magic number as to how big these communities should be, and every city had specific needs, but the Singaporean model[9] of transit-oriented, self-sufficient towns was used as a starting point.

Given the high density of Chinese cities, decentralised communities of 25,000 people could be planned at an actual 10 minutes' walking distance to all supporting amenities, therefore reducing the need for commuting. This meant that rather than the typical car-centred approach, human-scale street life could be reintroduced as a key element of the urban design.[10] The location and functions of the community hub within each cluster were fundamental in enabling each to develop a distinctive voice and preserve its own cultural identity. Additionally, more – and more diverse – amenities were proposed for these self-sufficient communities compared with the minimum set by the national planning code,[11] focusing especially on entertainment, sports and cultural facilities.

The clusters were also designed to break down the typical large land parcel sizes into smaller, more permeable and walkable blocks using passive security and landscaping instead of fences and gated communities. The landscape design was central to creating successful open spaces, with the distribution of green areas deliberately concentrated in courtyards and community gardens useable by all. Against the backdrop of virtualisation that has steadily shaped global societies right up until 2050, cities planned around community clusters have also provided much-needed physical space for social interaction.

This enhanced urban cluster model was essential to the implementation of community-scale low-carbon infrastructure that was relatively small and easy to manage and upgrade when new green technologies became competitive. This in turn allowed for a more localised approach to resources consumption, such as energy and waste, but also food production through community urban farming projects, boosting education and innovation and enabling sustainable lifestyle choices.

When planning cities in 2015, we knew at Arup that there was no simple solution to China's multifaceted urbanisation problems; real achievement came only when we started putting people first. ⌂

Shanghai's disappearing old neighbourhoods, 2012

top centre: The most vibrant communities are not necessarily the prettiest.

Shanghai residents raise their voice, 2014

top right: Local residents protest against a planned development in the centre of Shanghai that threatens their community.

Arup Associates, Sutong Science and Technology Park Masterplan, Nantong, China, 2012

below: Designing new cities with people in mind: the mixed-use community can easily reach the linear town centre on foot, while the two community centres provide key facilities and amenities for each residential cluster.

☐ Residential   ☐ Schools   ☐ Flexible Area   ☐ Public Green
▨ Mixed-Use   ■ Commercial   ☐ Water   ▨ Various Utilities

Typical segregated land use plan with functions grouped in separate zones.

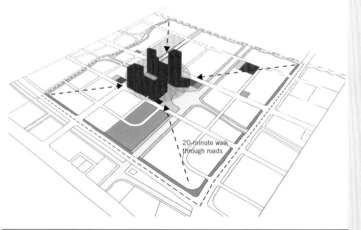

20-minute walk through roads

A residential cluster analysis system provides all key facilities and supporting amenities to the community accessible through a network of green corridors.

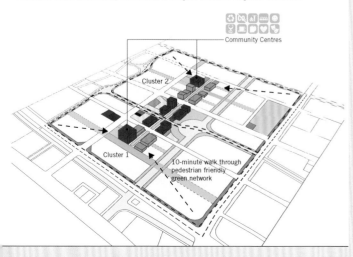

Community Centres

Cluster 2

Cluster 1

10-minute walk through pedestrian friendly green network

Notes

1. China's urban population was 308 million in the 1990s, 758 million in 2014, and is projected to be over a billion by 2050. Source: United Nations, Department of Economic and Social Affairs, Population Division, *World Urbanization Prospects: The 2014 Revision, Highlights* (ST/ESA/SER.A/352), p 21.
2. Alex Levinson and Kristen McDonald, 'Why Citizen Participation Should be Encouraged in China's 13th Five-year Plan', chinadialogue, 30 October 2014: www.chinadialogue.net/blog/7440-Why-citizen-participation-should-be-encouraged-in-China-s-13th-Five-Year-Plan/en.
3. Yuan Ren, Associate Professor, Institute of Population Research, Fudan University, 'NGOs, Public Participation and Urban Community Development: Social Reform in Local Urban Governance in China': http://mumford.albany.edu/chinanet/events/past_conferences/conferences/Yuan.doc.
4. Xinzhi Zhang, Wan-Ying Lin, 'Political Participation in an Unlikely Place: How Individuals Engage in Politics through Social Networking Sites in China', *International Journal of Communication*, 8, 2014, pp 21–42.
5. Across China, the forced eviction of old urban communities as well as rural villages was often characterised by episodes of violence and coercion by the authorities responsible for their eviction and relocation. See Jeffrey Hays, 'Land Grabs, Protests and Farmer's Rights in China', Facts and Details, April 2012: http://factsanddetails.com/china/cat9/sub63/item1109.html; Malcolm Moore, 'Chinese Setting Themselves on Fire to Protest Against Forced Evictions', *The Telegraph*, 11 October 2012: www.telegraph.co.uk/news/worldnews/asia/china/9599098/Chinese-setting-themselves-on-fire-to-protest-against-forced-evictions.html; and Josh Chin with Juliet Ye, 'China's Blood-Stained Property Map', China Real Time blog, *Wall Street Journal*, 29 October 2010: http://blogs.wsj.com/chinarealtime/2010/10/29/chinas-blood-stained-property-map/.
6. Jonathan Shieber, 'A Law to End Forced Demolitions', China Real Time blog, *Wall Street Journal*, 21 April 2011: http://blogs.wsj.com/chinarealtime/2011/04/21/a-law-to-end-forced-demolitions/.
7. Richard E Nisbett, *The Geography of Thought: How Asians and Westerners Think Differently...and Why*, Free Press/Simon & Schuster (New York), 2004, p 49.
8. Robert Gifford, 'The Consequences of Living in High-Rise Buildings', *Architectural Science Review*, 50, 1, 2007, pp 2–17.
9. Urban Redevelopment Authority, *Designing Our City, Planning for a Sustainable Singapore*: www.ura.gov.sg/skyline/skyline12/skyline12-03/special/URA_Designing%20our%20City%20Supplement_July12.pdf.
10. Liu Qin, 'China Must Stop Building Car-Centred Cities', chinadialogue, 6 October 2014: www.chinadialogue.net/blog/7366-China-must-stop-building-car-centred-cities/en and Tom Levitt, 'Chinese Cities "Feel the Loss of Streetlife and Community"', chinadialogue, 5 November 2012: www.chinadialogue.net/article/show/single/en/5291-Chinese-cities-feel-the-loss-of-streetlife-and-community-.
11. People's Republic of China national standard 'Urban Residential Area Planning Design Code' GB 50180-93 (Amendment Notice No 31, 2002).

Roberta L Bondar

Dust around V838
Monocerotis, 2002

As captured by the Hubble Space Telescope, the red supergiant star in the middle of the image illuminates an interstellar dusty cloud, likely ejected from the star in a previous explosion.

heaven on earth

'By 2050 we will have probed the universe even further, peeling back time as we strive for some sense of creation and meaning.' The world's first neurologist in space, **Roberta L Bondar**, who conducted international experiments on space mission STS 42 and has subsequently undertaken neurological research with NASA, urges us to look up and into space, which is set to remain a rich area of exploration, scientific investigation and wonder, with the discovery of new planets, light, patterns and materials on the not-so-distant horizon.

Tree islands, Wood
Buffalo National Park of
Canada, Alberta, 2014

Islands of trees are isolated from
each other by the highly alkaline
salty surface, grey with recent rain.
Red samphire or fleshy marsh
fingers line the wet edges of the
salt plains.

Winding river on salt
plains, Wood Buffalo
National Park of Canada,
Alberta, 2012

Six wood bison cross salty water
that has been forced to the
surface by impermeable bedrock.
Vegetarians, bison find the sodium
that plants cannot provide in the salt
plains, formed when underground
water evaporates.

Star-forming pillars in
the Carina Nebula, 2010

A composite of separate exposures
by the Hubble Space Telescope, this
image is 3.1 light years wide, while
the nebula itself is 7,500 light years
from Earth. The pillar of dust and gas
is 3 light years tall.

Out of the darkness of space, new things will touch the human eye. Even as our vision continues to be informed by compelling relationships of colour, texture, form and structure, concepts of empty space will also shift as we move beyond constraints that are imposed by contemporary knowledge.

The more we discover, the more we change our thinking of what is possible, and thus the greater the potential for creativity and innovation. In the search for new planets and with the discovery of previously unknown phenomena in the heavens, our outward view will continue to evolve our earthly world – the one will not exist without the other. The expressive aesthetic exists because of scientific enquiry.

Celestial objects have long been used in design to evoke a spiritual and futuristic connection. The Sun has figured in design and artistic expression throughout the human journey. By day we use sunlight to illuminate and shadows to contrast. We do not always remember that it is a nuclear power plant within a sculpted structure. And when we look up to the night sky, we are not always aware that we are seeing well beyond the Sun and into the past.

It is ironic that the images taken by the Hubble Space Telescope of light and form, so brilliant and unearthly, are of substances that probably have already morphed into another pattern. We just won't be alive long enough to see it. By 2050 we will have probed the universe even further, peeling back time as we strive for some sense of creation and meaning.

Swirls on Jupiter, meteor impacts creating new storms, hidden oceans of ice on Neptune's moon, even the far side of our own Moon have secrets. There are new and exciting patterns yet to be glimpsed, let alone incorporated in Earth objects and structures. The impact of space technology on our creative expression is truly a Möbius loop.

Given that experimental vertical take-off and landing rockets are a reality, it is not a stretch to slide towards a Flash Gordon-esque world. It is unlikely, however, that all civilisations on Earth will progress to the same place and at the same speed. Some may continue to leapfrog technology while incorporating a creative aesthetic that resonates with an evolving culture.

The scientific reality of space exploration can lead us into a dream-like state that engages our connectivity on emotional and spiritual levels. It is one thing to achieve a trip to Mars or to an asteroid; it is quite another to absorb the beauty of an environment caused by forces much different to those experienced on Earth. Halfway into 2100, new materials or more of those that are scarce on our planet could be mined and brought back here. What we hold precious may be mundane elsewhere, and what we hold commonplace may be unique. With discovery of new worlds, light, patterns, textures and materials, imaginations will just get bigger.

We have always looked to the heavens for answers. Perhaps that outward voyage will bring us back to Heaven on Earth in 2050. ∆

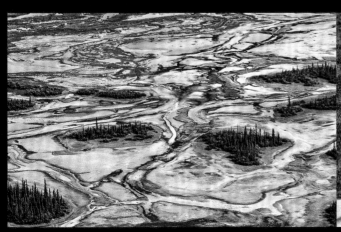

Shifting the focus from futuristic visions,
Alfredo Brillembourg and Hubert Klumpner
with **Alexis Kalagas** of interdisciplinary
design practice Urban-Think Tank urge us
to 'forget about utopia', for in the most part
the urban environment of 2050 is already
built. Architects' sights need to be set on the
sometimes grim and unfolding reality
of favelas and the world's informal cities.

El Sur
Global

Future Resilient City

Alfredo Brillembourg and Hubert Klumpner with Alexis Kalagas

Urban-Think Tank, Open Village, Shenzhen, Guangdong, China, 2015

An experimental prototype for a mixed-use open building that would support a sustainable vertical community.

In 1956, London's Whitechapel Gallery brought together the cultural avant-garde and pop sci-fi in its seminal exhibition 'This Is Tomorrow'. Opened by Robby the Robot, the fictional character from the film *Forbidden Planet,* released the same year, the show embodied the Space Age aesthetic and consumer fetishism of the era. But fantasies of a sleek, shiny future were soon superseded by the ominous noir of Jean-Luc Godard's *Alphaville* (1965) and bleak 'near-present' framing JG Ballard's fictional prophesies. The future was already here. Technology would not save us, but destroy us. The urban built environment became a sinister protagonist in this anxious narrative. Progressive monuments to modernity would leave a troubling psychological, social and environmental legacy. The city of tomorrow would look a lot like the city of today, just amplified.

This alarmism extends to our own crisis era.[2] But a darkening zeitgeist does not stem from questions of form or style. Whether in Caracas, Athens, Cape Town or Shenzhen, grim urban visions of the future reflect in part the failure of policy makers, architects and designers to conceive of the city as a place of equal opportunity. We no longer possess a universally applicable urban image, neither as a guiding cultural ideal nor as a model for intervention. In other words, forget about Utopia. Beyond the instant metropolises sprouting in China or the Gulf, much of the built environment of 2050 already exists. Yet as William McDonough argues, the city is both a natural object and a thing to be cultivated: 'Cities are organisms, and cities are designed – something lived and something dreamed.'[3] The informal city in particular is a city in a state of constant flux, expanding, reproducing and generating new uses. There is no 'final' product.

Embracing Fluidity

The pace and scale of urbanisation in places like Lagos or Mumbai suggests that whether or not they represent the terminal condition of the (post) modern city, they have plenty to teach us about the future. In his set of proposals for a 'New Athens Charter', Andrea Branzi depicts the 'city as a high-tech favela'.[4] An urban zone that avoids rigid solutions and fosters reversible structures that can be dismantled and transformed, accommodating new, unforeseen activities. Imagine a perpetually unfinished city. Buildings are mixed-use: workshops, light industry and agriculture are interlaced with residences, sports fields, schools and markets. Nodes of congregation are constantly moving and changing, adjusting to shifting influences and needs. Rhizomatic growth taps into both primitive and sophisticated materials and techniques. The city is alive 24 hours a day. If this seems like the ultimate nightmare, we see a potential mode of sustainability and tolerance.

What is the role of the architect in such a city? In the end there is both a struggle and a synergy between social realities and architectural ideas. Rather than imposing change, we must engage

As a prophet I have been
no better than anyone else;
my good fortune has been
due to the fact that I kept my
optimistic predictions
to myself and published
only the pessimistic ones.

— Lewis Mumford, quoted in Michael Hughes, *The Letters of Lewis Mumford and Frederic J Osborn*, 1971, p 97[1]

Paraisópolis favela, São Paulo,
Brazil, 2012

It is a common practice in Brazilian favelas to expand
a home incrementally as resources become available,
with each 'growing house' appearing perpetually
unfinished.

In the hope of generating additional income from tenants,
Joaquim is independently building an extra floor on his home.

Petare barrio, Caracas,
Venezuela, 2011

opposite: In Caracas, the informal hillside barrios
have expanded and reproduced like a complex
organism, housing approximately 60 per cent
of the city's population.

Seguros Caracas Estacionamiento,
Caracas, Venezuela, 2012

below: An existing parking structure now hosts
multiple additional programmes, including a
restaurant and cafeteria, clinic and offices.

real-world logic and attempt to provide prototypical solutions for urban
dwellers to give them better control over their evolving environments.
Yet the idea of the city as 'high-tech favela' also represents a composite
vision that presumes certain universal qualities identifiable in – and
radiating outward from – the world's emerging urban zones. It suggests
the potential for more unified design strategies. Of course, while
the future is always ahead, we act on past experience and present
assumptions. The only viable path forward is to establish a broad
framework and structure within which development can take place
according to the wishes and needs of the community it serves. An
architecture of adaptation, rather than ego.

Known Unknowns

Open building concepts were first popularised by Le Corbusier's Maison
Dom-ino (1914) in the wake of the devastation of the First World War.
But the Dutch architect, educator and theorist John Habraken took the
idea even further in the 1960s by imagining it as a means to anticipate
changing user demands and embed participation in the design process.
Advocating a radical alternative to the mass housing of the postwar
boom, he envisioned a future where architects would design building
frameworks while residents assumed responsibility for customised
infill development over time.[5] People ultimately make (and remake)
their own surroundings. Our urban future is antithetical to notions
of completeness or finality. It is what we discovered in Torre David.
It is what Habraken understood intuitively in his focus on resilience,
adaptability and transformability. A fundamental challenge is to
approach new design projects with a process of perpetual change in
mind – in short, to create open, flexible structures.

A number of contemporary developments evoke Habraken's ideas,
whether consciously or unconsciously. The Grundbau und Siedler (Basic
Building and Settlers) project by BeL Associates, for instance, was
designed and constructed for the 2013 Hamburg International Building
Exhibition (IBA) as a replicable pilot aimed at providing an adaptable
solution for DIY multifamily housing. A reinforced concrete skeleton
of five open floors provides the basic structural canvas for residents

Torre David, Caracas,
Venezuela, 2012

left: An unfinished 45-storey
skyscraper, the 'Tower of David'
became the improvised home to
more than 750 families living in a
self-organised community.

bottom: Residents transformed
empty shells into habitable living
quarters with many of the features
of conventional apartments, in
this case including a makeshift
mezzanine.

to then determine and complete their own living spaces. And from the perspective of adaptive reuse rather than new construction, the ongoing OCT-Loft redevelopment in Shenzhen by Urbanus has transformed vacant industrial relics into a mixed-use artistic and cultural node. Urban-Think Tank's Fábrica de Cultura project in Barranquilla, Colombia (2015) extends these principles of flexibility and customisation to social infrastructure in a tropical environment, prioritising open, versatile spaces that can cater to the specialised technical needs of students, but also serve the wider community.

The work of Urban-Think Tank has centred on the dynamic cities of the *Sur Global* (Global South). These are spaces of ordered delirium and yawning inequality, defined by a fluid mode of development and a population that grows with every driving impulse. If cities are simultaneously lived and dreamed, then our task in imagining the teeming metropolises of 2050 is to envisage how social needs can best be translated into physical form. Despite the infinite adaptability of informality, we cannot afford to let the future city as 'hi-tech favela' fall hostage to the same mechanisms that spatialise and materialise uneven development today. Sustainability has both an environmental and social dimension. In the same way that urban migrants are attracted by the promise of security as well as upward mobility, open building concepts are ultimately about achieving an elusive balance between stability and self-initiated change. A design mechanism to create and foster productive urban growth. △

Notes
1. Michael Hughes (ed), *The Letters of Lewis Mumford and Frederic J Osborn,* Adams & Dart (Bath), 1971, p 97.
2. David Cunningham and Alexandra Warwick, 'Unnoticed Apocalypse: The Science Fiction Politics of Urban Crisis', *CITY,* 17, 4, 2013, pp 433–4.
3. William McDonough, 'Something Lived, Something Dreamed: Principles and Poetics in Urban Design', in Tigran Haas (ed), *New Urbanism and Beyond: Designing Cities for the Future,* Rizzoli (New York), 2008, p 61.
4. Andrea Branzi, 'For a Post-Environmentalism: Seven Suggestions for a New Athens Charter', in Mohsen Mostafavi and Gareth Doherty (eds), *Ecological Urbanism,* Lars Müller (Zurich), 2010, p 110.
5. John Habraken, *Supports: An Alternative to Mass Housing,* The Architectural Press (London), 1972.

Urban-Think Tank,
Fábrica de Cultura,
Barranquilla, Colombia,
2015

Above: Here, the architects worked in close collaboration with the Inter-American Development Bank, Swiss government, ETH Zurich engineers and local partners to create a flexible, open building for a district arts school.

Left: The 'culture factory' has been designed as a replicable prototype that could be customised to suit other environmental and social contexts.

Capt Nemo D

Jules Verne's Captain Nemo in *Twenty Thousand Leagues Under the Sea* (1870) was the first marine conservationist, battling against his fellow humans to protect the wildlife of the oceans. Here, the deeply passionate marine ecologist and National Geographic Explorer-in-Residence **Enric Sala** enlists the help of his hero to capture what might be in store for ocean life in 2050.

Enric Sala

The largest bank
account on earth,
2050

The yellow areas on the map
show a 2050 scenario, with
50 per cent of the ocean in
'no-take' marine reserves
where fishing is prohibited.
The goal of the reserve
network is to restore ocean
life so that it can continue
to produce returns we can
enjoy – from more sustainable
fishing outside the reserves,
to insurance against climate
change – keeping our
environment and us healthy.

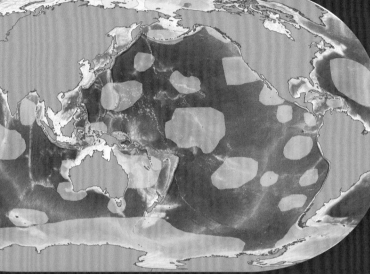

ain
a's
'
r ream

When the seas have been depleted of whales and seals ... we shall then have our waters cluttered with octopi, jellyfish, and squids, which will create hotbeds of infection in the absence of those huge mammals, whose stomachs were intended by God to keep the oceans clean! – Jules Verne, *Twenty Thousand Leagues Under the Sea,* 1870[1]

These words come to me often when at sea. They are from Jules Verne's visionary book written in 1870. In a story that has captivated me for decades, Captain Nemo commands a futuristic submarine with a loyal crew in a battle against humans who mercilessly exploit the oceans. Nemo was the first marine conservationist in history. It took scientists more than a hundred years to understand what he already knew: that man has been killing and consuming everything large and, unintentionally, fostering the growth of small animals and microbes.

AD 2015: Somewhere in the South Pacific

My fingers distractedly caressed a dog-eared copy of Verne's book, a faithful companion on all my ocean expeditions, as I looked outside the window of my cabin. My ship was at anchor, silent but for the slapping of small waves against her sides. All was quiet, until a blinding light and an explosion threw me from my chair. As I ran above deck, there was an unmistakable glow on the beach, in the shape of a giant sleigh. A silhouette materialised into view, like an apparition.

Without thinking I jumped on our Zodiac, always at the ready, turned her nose towards the light and hit the throttle. When I landed the Zodiac and slithered onto the warm sand, my heart beat as though I had been running a marathon.

'How is the ocean?', a deep, male voice boomed as soon as I was upright. His face, in view now, was tan, tough, with an immaculate black beard.

'What?' I said, confused.

'I'm Captain Nemo,' he barked impatiently. 'How is the ocean?'

Yes, I could see it now: he looked like the Captain Nemo illustration in my book. Nemo came closer and grabbed me by the shoulders.

'I've come from 1870 to see how the ocean is, and I don't have much time. Is ocean life safe now?' he asked.

Well, I was sure of one thing: if this was indeed Captain Nemo he would not be happy to see what we had done to the oceans since his time. But only a fool would want to suffer his ire. Besides, I had dedicated my life to restoring ocean life, and didn't feel that I should carry the burden of the actions of past generations. I mustered my strength and pushed him back towards his time machine.

'Come back to this spot in 2050,' I implored while steering him to the threshold of the craft. 'We need more time. Trust me.'

Our eyes met and he understood. He exhaled heavily, stared for a moment longer, and closed the door.

AD 2050: Same Location

I had been waiting months now for his return. For many years I wasn't sure whether I wanted him to come back. But now there was so much to show him.

The flash shocked me again as his ship materialised on my deck. He looked just as he did in 2015. In his time machine, perhaps only seconds had passed. For me, I was now 35 years older, with a lifetime of work behind me.

'Captain Nemo, welcome back. Follow me,' I said, confidently. We went down to the dive deck and donned full-helmet diving re-breathers. As soon as we jumped into the water, 10 grey reef sharks surrounded us. I could feel my heartbeat double, not due to the sharks' presence, but because I was about to show Nemo how the ocean had recovered from too much fishing and pollution.

Looking down, the coral reef was hidden by the thousands of fish schooling above it. Yellow snappers with delicate blue lines along their sides swam between two manta rays gracefully flying, and a giant grouper, large as a bicycle, made little fish panic and dart away. We saw a lush garden of corals of intricate complexity, a forest of calcium carbonate, and red sea fans swaying with the slight underwater current near giant clams with impossible electric blue and green mantles.

A metre-long red snapper approached Nemo, hit his mask, and then bolted away.

Life was everywhere. Although I spent my life diving, every time I jumped in pristine water I was filled with awe and wonder,

like the little kid who discovers something wonderful in his backyard. Seeing nature in its purest state made me the happiest man on earth. I turned to Nemo, and saw him crying inside his helmet.

Back on board our ship, he asked whether the ocean was as rich everywhere.

'Yes, but it took us a long time to help everyone see that we could either enjoy a life of abundance or one of misery if we continued to pollute and deplete the ocean of fish,' I said. 'Eventually, world leaders worked together to avert catastrophe.[2] We focused on three main things.

'We gave half of the ocean back to nature for her to manage. We finally realised that the ocean does a far better job than we ever could, at first renewing herself and then remaining healthy and productive. Today, half the ocean is a no-take reserve, a huge savings account that helps to replenish the other half, which we continue to fish and use. We catch the same amount of fish as before, but with less effort and half the fishing boats.'

'What about ocean farming?' Nemo queried, 'something I developed in the late 1800s.'

'We built upon your vision, and now ocean farming produces delicious seaweed, invertebrates and fish without damaging the ocean environment. Our ocean farms are complete ecosystems that recycle their own waste and clean the waters around them,' I said proudly. 'Then we applied this concept to our industries. Now there is no more waste, and no more plastic ending up in the ocean.'

'Plastic?', Nemo asked, frowning.

'It was after your time, Captain, but horrid during mine. Never mind, we now follow a "cradle to cradle" approach to everything we do. Every material is reused *ad infinitum*. We just needed to imitate how non-human ecosystems worked. No pollution enters the ocean anymore.'

'You have no idea how relieved I am,' said Nemo. 'I feel like all my work was worth the sacrifice, my sailing away from the mad world of more than a billion people.'

'Captain, when you came 35 years ago we were already at seven billion people. We were consuming everything just to keep up with that mad human population explosion. And yes, we had some losses. We put so many pollutants in the atmosphere and heated it up so much that your once impenetrable Arctic Ocean is now free of sea ice in the summer. But right after you left, we began learning how to harness the energy of the sun efficiently, and invented machines re-creating the reactions that occur in its centre to produce unlimited energy. The smokestacks of England in the late 19th century are only found on the canvas of paintings. We expect the Arctic sea ice to reappear in the summer again within a few decades.'

'That's very different from my perfect dream for the ocean,' Nemo said, sadly.

'Maybe, but think about this. We have been able to protect half of the ocean and manage our activities in the other half intelligently. The waters and the atmosphere are cleaner, and the oceans that keep us alive are getting healthier,' I said with a smile. 'At one point I was pessimistic about ever accomplishing anything significant. But we made it. It was worth the fight. And your vision inspired me and many others to do the right thing.'

Having heard that, the good Captain stood, gave me a bear hug, and recited a passage from my favorite book as he entered his time machine: 'There is hope for the future. When the world is ready for a new and better life, all this will someday come to pass, in God's good time.'[3] ⌀

The road to ocean recovery, 2015–50

In 2015, coral reefs suffered too much fishing, pollution and warming – and consequently a quarter of them were gone. A few decades after protecting reefs from direct human impacts such as fishing and pollution, they recovered their fish and corals, bringing back the health and magic of a thriving ocean. The endpoint of recovery occurred when the large predators, the sharks, became the kings of the ocean once again.

Notes
1. Jules Verne, *Twenty Thousand Leagues Under the Sea*, Penguin (London), 1994, p 339.
2. See pristineseas.org for a description of how the author and the National Geographic Pristine Seas team are inspiring world leaders to protect the last wild places in the ocean.
3. From the film version of Verne's novel: http://en.wikiquote.org/wiki/20,000_Leagues_Under_the_Sea_%28film%29.

Molly Wright Steenson

Bricked House

How Code and Law Can Lock You Out

mmmm (Alberto Alarcón, Emilio Alarcón,
Ciro Márquez and Eva Salmerón), Brick Car,
'2 x 1' exhibition, Matadero, Madrid, 2010

Pixilated in place, a bricked car in the most literal of senses:
a 5-tonne vehicle by the Spanish artist collective mmmm,
constructed by a brick mason and an engineer.

Could we be unwittingly divesting too much control in technology? In so doing, could we be sleepwalking into a future in which our personal assets are no longer ours, but all too easily relinquished by the bank or mortgage company? **Molly Wright Steenson**, an assistant professor in the School of Journalism and Mass Communication at the University of Wisconsin-Madison, thinks so. She evokes an arresting vision of a close future in which our smartphones and the operating systems integrated within our cars and homes become our friend-enemy, immediately locking us out when they are no longer programmed to respond directly to our touch.

etaphorically speaking, the bricked car renders itself inaccessible to
user, leaving her locked in place and unresponsive.

My house got 'bricked'. That's what we used to call it when you altered your smartphone's operating system against your service contract: it turned itself into an unresponsive brick. But in this case, it was my house. My rent was an hour late, it was after midnight and my door wouldn't open. Without an immediate money transfer, it wouldn't let me in. The only choice was an explicit transaction: making an immediate payment or standing out in the cold and wetting my pants.

Smartphones were the more innocuous of our objects to lock up, but things got much more insidious when our mobility and security were compromised.[1] In 2015, cars already glide to a halt on busy highways when their owners miss payments, thanks to the smart ignition and shutdown devices installed, largely, in those of people with undesirable financial circumstances—their only choice. But what if we zoom into a more microscopic scale, to devices embedded in the human body? When a medical device, for example an insulin pump, suddenly stops delivering vital medication to its patient due to an insurance hiccup?

Mercedes-Benz W 113
'Pagoda', 1963–71

It is easy to miss the old interfaces of the traditional car, with ordinary ignition switches that turned on and off the way the driver expected.

Many things get bricked these days as law and internet protocols intersect the architecture of the objects and technologies that surround us. It's called 'embedded governance', or in shorter terms, 'code as law'.

Many things get bricked these days as law and internet protocols intersect the architecture of the objects and technologies that surround us.[2] It's called 'embedded governance', or in shorter terms, 'code as law'. At issue is how these so-called 'smart' object architectures target various constituencies. In reality, someone of better means might be able to negotiate an hour or even a day more to make a payment, certainly for her own personal safety.[3] But an ordinary person when locked out of the house, or left at the side of the road, could find herself with nothing to discuss. The danger here is that devices, objects, infrastructures and technologies step in to take the place of law. They become enforcement mechanisms without nuance or negotiation.

It's one thing for this mediation to take place where we can see it, such as the security apparatus in place at a fence or a border,[4] but quite another when it confronts us at the scale of our most personal architectures. As Helen Nissenbaum writes: 'Technology mediates and gives texture to certain kinds of private relationships; it weighs in on the side of one vested interest over others.'[5] It is unlikely to favour the person with the bricked house, phone or pacemaker.

On their own, objects, technologies and computer algorithms are poor stand-ins for law. They perform a few tasks well and others much less so, and they increasingly hide their intentions from our view. The finer the grain of these questions, and the closer to our bodies this governance gets, the itchier the consequences. I miss my old house with its metal keys. I miss my old car with its quaint ignition. I even miss parking tickets. But I especially miss the notion of the objects around me being open to negotiation, and not imbued with laws that leave us bricked. ⚙

Embedded governance

By enmeshing laws and rules with objects, embedded governance provides barriers to the users of everyday objects.

Notes
1. Michael Corkery and Jessica Silver-Greenberg, 'Good Luck Moving That Car', *New York Times*, 24 September 2014: http://dealbook.nytimes.com/2014/09/24/miss-a-payment-good-luck-moving-that-car.
2. Jake Dunagan, 'Designer Governance', *Futures*, 44, 2012, p 840.
3. Kashmir Hill, 'People With Bad Credit Can Buy Cars, But They Are Tracked And Have Remote-Kill Switches', *Forbes*, 25 September 2014: www.forbes.com/sites/kashmirhill/2014/09/25/starter-interrupt-devices.
4. Helen Nissenbaum, 'From Preemption to Circumvention: If Technology Regulates, Why Do We Need Regulation (and Vice Versa)?', *Berkeley Technology Law Journal*, 26, 2011, p 1374.
5. *Ibid*, p 1375.

Franz Oswald

Looking Back

on a

Radical Idea

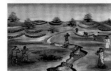

The Buranest Cooperative Rural New Town
Amhara, Ethiopia

Does the megacity have to inevitably represent the urban future? Could the seemingly onward march of rapid and large-scale urbanisation in fact be interceded by 2050 with the development of more, smaller local towns? Architect and Professor Emeritus at ETH Zurich **Franz Oswald** is the founding president of the New Ethiopian Sustainable Town (NESTown). He describes here how he and a small group of Ethiopian and Swiss professionals intervened in 2010 in urban migration by founding the new farming community of Buranest in the Amhara region of Ethiopia, and what the impact of this invention might be 35 years hence.

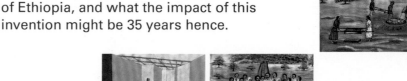

Notes
1. See http://esa.un.org/
unpd/wup/Highlights/
WUP2014-Highlights.pdf
http://esa.un.org/unpd/
wup/Highlights/WUP2014-
Highlights.pdf, pp 1 and 8,
figure 2.
2. See http://esa.un.org/
unpd/wup/Highlights/
WUP2014-Highlights.pdf
http://esa.un.org/unpd/
wup/Highlights/WUP2014-
Highlights.pdf, p 9.
3. Idea and concept:
Professor Franz Oswald,
ETH Zurich; Architect Peter
Schenker, Bern; Professor
Fasil Giorghis, EiABC/AAU;
Professor Dr Dieter Läpple,
Regional Economy, HCU
Hamburg.
4. Advice and Support:
Professor Dr Marc Angélil,
ETH Zurich; Professor Dr
Philippe Block, ETH Zurich;
Professor Dr Hans Hurni,
geographer, University
of Bern; Dominik
Langenbacher, Swiss
Ambassador, Nairobi;
Monika Oswald, Bern;
Peter Schmid, cooperatives
expert, Zurich; Benjamin
Stähli, Town Project
Coordinator, Bahir Dar;
Dr Roland Walthert,
Principal Engineer,
Wettingen; Helawe Yoseph,
Ambassador of Ethiopia,
Tel Aviv; Zegeye Cherenet,
architect and Director elect
EiABC/AAU.
5. Mastewai Tesfaye is
a fictitious character.
Any resemblance to a
known individual of the
same name is completely
coincidental.

The seemingly non-stop urbanising landslide of humanity began well before the turn of the century. In 1900, 20 per cent of our population were urbanites; by 2000 it was just shy of 50 per cent and now, in 2050, it is about 70 per cent.[1] One might not naturally have picked the Ethiopian farmer as holding the solution to the global challenge of mass population migration from rural areas to ill-prepared and overcrowded capital cities. One should. Because on land in the farming village community of Bura on Lake Tana, in the Amhara region, a self-sustaining town founded in 2010 has resulted in long-term improvements in the everyday lives of citizens across the Horn of Africa. In 2050 it is an exemplar of a multi-generational, sustainable and thriving community. And this is vital because Africa has had the highest rate of urbanisation in the world since 2020.[2]

This real-life experiment was a cooperative new town – named Buranest – built for farmers, by farmers, with input from farmers – all without external investors. The idea was the brainchild of a small group of Ethiopian and Swiss professionals[3] who dreamt up the New Ethiopian Sustainable Town (NESTown) model to face head on the staggering urban population growth projections, environmental destruction concerns, degrading social cohesion and simply keep strong adolescents, capable of working the beautiful land, in the countryside, instead of them migrating to larger cities. The Amhara government saw the value for its citizens, and championed the idea. The small team rapidly expanded to include a wide variety of experts in Europe and in Ethiopia.[4]

At the Biennial Conference of Cooperative Towns held in Dhaka, Bangladesh, in 2050, the president of the Ethiopian delegation, Mastewal Tesfaye,[5] a farmer's son from Bura and former Buranest Town Core Coordinator, spoke eloquently about why this model town has since been replicated throughout Ethiopia: 'It's helpful to understand the growth of this rural area. Today Addis Zemen, Yifag and Buranest have 235,000 inhabitants, a staggering increase from the 45,000 in 2007. Buranest has grown the most.'

When asked why, Tesfaye didn't hesitate: 'Cooperation in all municipal activities is why. Everyone participates, so there is an unmistakable identity. In the central town square, in the shade of a tree whose canopy stretches 40 metres (130 feet), people of both sexes and all ages meet. They talk, make decisions, share bread, make music, dance or simply sit quietly. You feel the pulse of the town beating strongly.'

Agriculture is the heart of Buranest. Each household has a parcel of land, and shares the rainwater that is collected from roofs and stored in wells, with neighbours. Cooperative production and storage give the inhabitants a secure source of food and water. Thoughtfully designed infrastructure with measured construction upon the land ensures both steady employment and protection against the elements.

'We've moved away from exploiting the landscape,' Tesfaye continued. 'We do everything purposefully, including planting millions of seedlings from local tree nurseries. Now water flows all year in the river basins.' As a result, despite the increased population, groundwater quality, water supply and agricultural yield have improved. People have even accepted the necessity of relocating their livestock.

However, Tesfaye admitted that it has taken time to make an impact on people: 'Individuals tend not to believe in quality through cooperation until they experience it themselves. The synergy of cooperation and balance, of do-it-yourself and trade, of people using their own funds and others receiving financial assistance, and the linking of natural and social systems took a while to take root. And now it is clearly blossoming.' He noted that it also took time to integrate the new towns into the broader national systems.

Construction work on the south-to-north rail connection with Buranest Station was dropped in 2027 due to the expanding network of roads and electrically powered transportation. 'It sounds paradoxical that we Ethiopians are culturally slow, but are quick to draw an innovative advantage from complex industrial products,' explained Tesfaye. 'We widened the two-lane regional road from Bahir Dar to Gonder to four lanes, with conductor strips for driverless vehicles.' There is enough hydroelectric, solar and wind energy that electric power made in Ethiopia drives domestic use and export. Tesfaye is clearly proud: 'For us, self-sufficiency – from nutrition to mobility and self-empowerment, from healthcare to education – remains embedded in both our history and landscape.'

Peace is the ultimate by-product of the Buranest experiment for Tesfaye: 'After epochs of killing and devastation, my generation was the first that had a chance to live out its years of study and travel in times of peace. My stints in Somalia and South Sudan have taught me how fragile such times are. That is why I made this commitment to new cooperative towns. They are an enduring attempt to build peace together, to share and give our young hope for a better future.'

The Buranest Charter
A Roadmap for a New Town

Any new town needs a few items to start: people, land, capital and an urban model. But success hinges on a politically agreed-upon strategy or charter. The charter used for Buranest consists of seven propositions relating to the way townspeople perceive their role in living together both outwardly and inwardly; the creative driving forces of urban dynamism in terms of ecology, energy, exchange and education; and the aesthetic material construct of urban architecture in the landscape.

Proposition 01

The town governs autonomously and acts with solidarity

The town is an enterprising corporation that produces income and resources from its own initiatives, competences, diversity and density of inhabitants. It follows the principles of autonomy and self-reliance. Participation and the balancing of resources and yields are openly discussed and equitably governed through interaction between individuals and community.

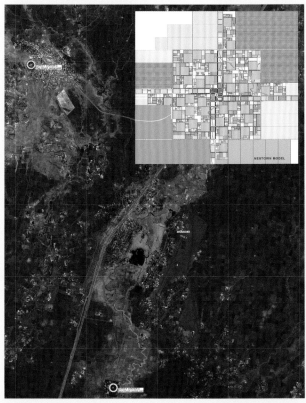

Proposition 02

The town sustains itself by self-defined urban quality and self-sufficiency

Self-defined urban quality is the competence to balance and integrate different needs and changing situations in the everyday life of the inhabitants. The criteria are chosen and applied by mutual agreement. The town seeks to cover its resource needs with a high degree of self-supply. The aim is congruence between given resources within its own periphery and the required resources for its own existence.

Proposition 03

The town controls its metabolism and offers all basic urban activities

Food production, work, housing, transport, communication and cleaning are jointly operated within the urban metabolism. They are sources of income. The town adjusts the flow of goods and material, including capital and information technology, to maintain equilibrium. It develops its cooperative urban identity from continually balancing new enterprises and resources.

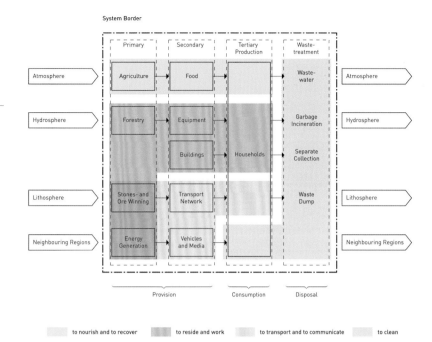

Proposition 04

The town lives from renewable resources and generates its own energy

The town transforms the forces of sun, water, soil and air to produce energy. It builds and operates its distribution network, invents alternative productions or applications of energy facilitating the human workload and supporting growth and diversity. A hybrid culture of tradition and high tech is applied to the benefit of urban added value.

Proposition 05

The town develops free exchange internally and externally

The town maintains routes and procedures of free exchange. The infrastructure is coordinated in a network and sustained cooperatively. It swaps materials and goods, experiences and values. New ideas and opportunities, as well as renewed demand for goods and services emerge.

Proposition 06

The town educates as practice and laboratory

The town learns from experience and hands this knowledge down to others. It incorporates production and application of knowledge, trial and development, imitation and invention. It offers permanent training.

Everyone participates, so there is an unmistakable identity.

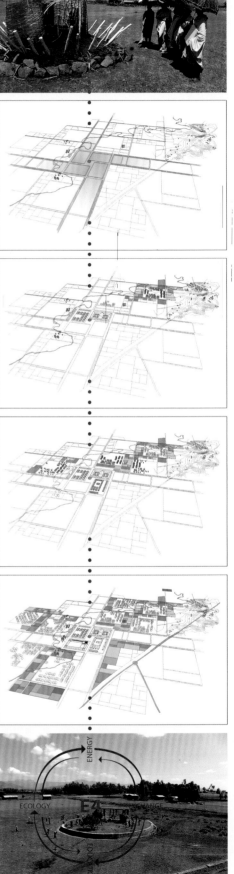

Proposition 07

The town has open institutions and gardens

The town, cooperatively built by the inhabitants, grows from the town core with a centre square and four nuclei based around ecology, energy, exchange and education. Growth is approved within time periods to allow later discussion and adjustment. Local resources, tools and the abilities of the inhabitants are used. The town form expresses the ownership of the inhabitants, creating comforting beauty. ⌀

In memory of Peter Schenker, 1947–2014

The Generous City

Author and biologist **Janine Benyus** is co-founder of Biomimicry 3.8, an innovation consultancy that brings brilliant ideas – informed by millions of years of evolution – to the design table. Here she envisages the urban environment in 2050, as one that is as generous as the natural forest expelling clean air and purified water.

You are in a translucent jet, gliding silently over a forested wilderness. You watch sunlight streak through the canopy and imagine how it feels to be under the boughs: pure air, silvery streams, fragrant soils and a calliope of birdsong. Everything that enters that forest – wind and water, and you – is renewed and refreshed by the life within. A forest creates goodness and then gifts it away.

Moments later, the scene shifts to streetscapes and skyscrapers, an urban home for millions. Here, too, you find cool air, clean water, fertile soil and a thrumming community that fits seamlessly into its watershed. It is 2050, and the city is as generous as the wildland next door.

This benevolence is by design. Thirty years ago, the city challenged itself to become a net producer of ecosystem services. Using healthy local ecosystems as their model, citizens adopted ecological performance standards – storing and purifying as much water as the native ecosystem, sequestering as much carbon, building as much soil, cleaning as much air, and more. To prove it possible right here and right now, ecologists drew the metrics (x litres of water, x tons of carbon) from current rather than historical reference habitats. Scenario simulators helped planners, architects and infrastructure engineers choose designs with a high 'generosity score'. Biomimicry helped them embed genius loci into their designs – animating the very bones and

> Scenario simulators helped planners, architects and infrastructure engineers choose designs with a high 'generosity score'.

Janine Benyus

Building skins that breathe like a tree

opposite left: Leaves do it all – harvesting energy, capturing fog, releasing oxygen, dissipating heat, and at the end of their life, fertilising soil that will give rise to new solar cells. The perfect model for a building skin.

A city that cleans water like a wetland

centre: A biomimetic city harvests, stores, purifies and slowly releases the same quantities of water as local wetlands. It takes a village to be part of the water cycle.

Pulling our ecological weight

right: To function like a forest, the whole city – built infrastructure and green ecostructure – works together to produce clean air, regulate climate, build soil and nurture biodiversity. It is more than benign; it is benevolent.

skin and organs of the city with the evolved wisdom of local organisms.

Decades later, the city is self-sufficient in food, water and energy, yet productive enough to give back to the rest of the biome. Homes and offices have ventilating skins that triple-cleanse the air, releasing oxygen and sequestering carbon dioxide in building materials. Absorptive sidewalks and plazas store water during storms, using peristaltic motion to slowly release it back to aquifers. Undulating roof canopies return water vapour to rain clouds, nourishing drier communities downwind. The brownfields are abloom, and roadways have sprouted linear parks. It is a city in a forest and a forest in a city, embroidered with

strands of migratory paths and agricultural corridors that mend the region whole.

A Cambrian explosion of innovation was needed to meet these goals, but luckily, as the city densified it became exponentially more creative. People say we are close to retiring the last landfill and celebrating the Great Drawdown, the removal of excess carbon from our atmosphere. Our manufacturing has shifted from giant factories to design-and-print shops on every other corner, bringing the safe and circular economy back home. Somehow we have squeezed through an evolutionary knothole.

Thirty years ago, staring into a climate abyss, we decided to come home to this

planet. We decided to be truly vernacular and it changed how we dreamt of ourselves as a species. It made us students of the natural world; partners rather than dominators. It made us reconsider what cities are for and what aspirational vows can conjure.

Our cities are as natural as nests, we realised. The more they function like native pinelands and prairies, taiga and tundra, the more lush and liveable they become. We are a part of nature, and our cities can create goodness too. And then, as generous as grasslands, they can gift it away. ⌂

Text © 2015 John Wiley & Sons Ltd. Images: p 120(l) © Jung Hsuan/Shutterstock; p 120(r) © Vladimir Melnikov/ Shutterstock; p 121 © iurii/Shutterstock

To a Curator of Beautiful and Healthy Lives

A Note to Myself

How might architectural thinking and processes shift over the next 35 years? How might the architect's role be redefined with shifting ethical values? Could the architect be viewed as less of a design professional and more of a curator engaged in the development of healthy holistic environments, catering for all of society's needs? **DaeWha Kang**, an architect from 2050, writes to his earlier self, critiquing the work that he undertook in independent practice and as a design director at Zaha Hadid Architects in the mid-2010s. He describes how his design methodologies have evolved in the intervening years.

DaeWha Kang Design,
Saemaeul-2 pavilion sketch,
Seoul, South Korea,
2015

Architectural structure provides
a framework for an ever-shifting
composition of lanterns that provide
light, heat, sound and information in
and among the endless fields of rice.

Dear DaeWha,

Hello from 2050! I am writing to you as a kind of reverse time capsule; perhaps these are ruminations from my early days[1] or even a critique of myself. Perhaps this is a chance to give you some hints for your future and to charge you with some confidence for the great challenges you will face.

First of all, architects have finally secured the idea of moving beyond physical environmental sustainability, and focused on human and societal wellbeing. Most of us evolved from the model of the architect as a suffering artist who created a large-scale inhabitable sculpture to be turned over to the owner on opening day and abandoned at the opening ceremony. This yielded to the more modern and profitable notion of the architect as a curator of a beautiful and healthy life. We now are again designing environments and buildings for all strata of society and are continuing to collaborate with our clients through the inhabitation, use and reuse of their assets. We focus on constant rejuvenation to make our lives ever more healthy and rich. By finding ways to actually measure the benefit to health, productivity and society, we have found that people are willing to engage us more often and pay us much more for truly outstanding design.

DaeWha Kang Design, Saemaeul-2 city sketch Seoul, South Korea, 2015

In this development outside of Seoul, historically agricultural land symbiotically interfaces with media, publishing and technological research. A new class of productive urbanism and landscape bridges the gap between the old and new.

FILM STUDIOS   POP-UP PAVILIONS   CANAL
SCULPTURES IN FIELDS   HOUSING AND OFFICES
ACTIVE RICE FIELDS   PRODUCTIVE CIVIC LANDSCAPE   DEVELOPABLE SITES
SEMICONDUCTOR FACTORIES   SERPENTINE PEDESTRIAN NETWORK

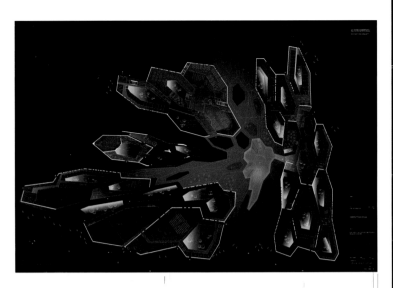

This concept of architectural practice is what led you to start your own studio so long ago. It forms the core of your philosophy even to this day. Finding the way to marry those ambitions with your deep passion for beauty, innovation and wisdom has taken you the better part of a generation. It was good you just got on with it, because you certainly needed every moment you had.

In 2009, for the King Abdullah Petroleum Studies and Research Center (KAPSARC) in Riyadh, the Saudi government asked for an iconic building that would stand as the highest exemplar of sustainable design. At Zaha Hadid's office you proposed an approach where sustainability was not achieved simply through technology applied onto the building (a sort of green bling), but through the holistic consideration of form as well. This was an instinct you developed in childhood, surrounded by nature and nestled between the Pacific Ocean and the Cascade Mountains of Oregon. In nature, every articulation and every form has a purpose. Nature's beautiful machine, with its intricate simplicity, subtly embeds long-term intelligence and sustainability within the form, not just applying it on top as a 'technology'.

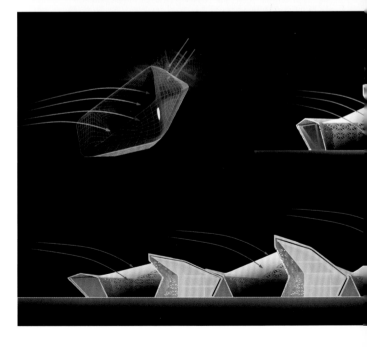

This natural approach to form is something that has been an important thread in the many years after KAPSARC. That design was a turning point for you, with dozens of courtyards collecting the cold desert air in the night. Each was sculpted and formed to progressively catch the cooling northern wind while shading the space from the strong southern and western sun. The wind caught by those shapes extended the usable time of the courtyards from six to nine months of the year, having a great impact on the daily lives of the researchers.

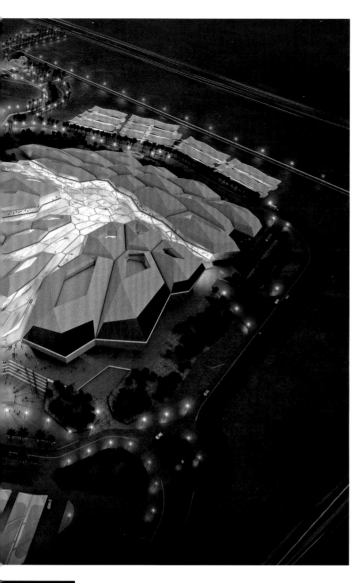

Zaha Hadid Architects,
King Abdullah Petroleum Studies
and Research Center (KAPSARC),
Riyadh, Saudi Arabia,
2015

above: The research centre is a collection of five buildings that share a common architectural language, responding to the sun and wind of the desert environment.

top left: The plan shows the strong emphasis on sheltered courtyards and shaded open space between the KAPSARC buildings.

left: The form of the building is designed to capture the cooling northern wind while shading from the strong southern and western sun.

right: Sheltered courtyards throughout the buildings give residents and visitors constant access to beautiful outdoor spaces, even in the extreme desert climate.

At the time you worked with Arup to employ cutting-edge simulations of computational fluid dynamics (CFD) on the building form, and ray-traced daylighting analysis in an iterative design process. Looking back, that was the key moment when you turned to science and empirical analysis to underpin your work. Our stated vision of employing beautiful and innovative design to measurably improve human wellbeing grew out of that experimental approach.

Over the years that work has borne fruit at all scales. Your studio was built on a philosophy of design, architecture, environment and wellbeing – from the products that we touch with our bodies to the architecture that we inhabit, to the city and landscape that surrounds us. And so the KAPSARC investigation at the building scale was just the beginning of a pursuit that subsequently applied this combination of aesthetics and empirical study to minute details of window frames that act as airfoils, up to the full-city daylighting analysis and CFD simulations that led to far more healthy and beautiful urban environments. And more importantly, we now model and monitor the movement of people and activity in relation to the sun and the wind, and the whole dance is beautifully choreographed through architecture and urban design (Bill Hillier and his 'space syntax' was just the beginning).

This broadening of scope and blurring of boundaries between the micro and macro, the hand-held and urban scale, has been one of the great changes of the last 35 years, and the test bed for so much innovation. Buildings, furniture, clothing and smaller things like phones and cameras and watches have all blended into a living network that constantly interacts with us and communicates with all its other elements. Design truly is choreography, and every element of our physical environment cradles and embraces us, nurturing our bodies and uplifting our souls. Design is now sensitively tuned to all the rhythms of life and nature.

You designed KAPSARC for a 60-year lifespan, and the toggle fixings on the glass-fibre reinforced concrete panels were intended to allow for easy removal and replacement of the facade when needed. You would have done well to follow more closely the work of William McDonough and Michael Braungart, and consider how those panels could have a life after this building. The weight of the panels is also enormous, and over the last three and a half decades Achim Menges and his atelier have developed increasingly durable, lightweight materials that are built directly from fibres, using material only where it is needed.

In fact, we don't design buildings with conventional ideas of longevity any more at all. All of the elements are detailed for different lifespans appropriate to their role, and the greater part of our effort goes to finding materials that can be upcycled for very little energy cost. In this way our thinking has moved beyond the idea of buildings as objects. We rather think of our cities as closed-loop systems, where one outdated building component immediately finds its use in another industry and another place.

The facade of a building is much more like the leaves shed from a tree every autumn than like a permanent piece of metal or concrete sculpture. Architecture students today are just as likely to study Sankey diagrams and Howard Odum's systems ecology as they are to study the structures and mechanical systems you studied in your time. Of course, all of this has been very good commercially, since the business model is about architecture as a continuous service, rather than something that each client tends to experience only once or twice in their lives.

Innovation is what allows us to flourish.

Space Syntax,
London Spatial
Accessibility Model,
London,
2015

Space Syntax uses computational analysis to evaluate the connectivity of paths, influencing human movement through the city and the socio-economic performance of places.

Wisdom is about making the right choices. What kind of stewards are we of our environment, resources and energy? Are we focusing our energy on work that truly makes the world a better place for today and tomorrow? Are we making everyone's lives richer through the choices we make and the environments we create? Wellbeing is the core of your practice, and you have never forgotten the importance of the human being.

Innovation is what allows us to flourish. Growth and progress are most easily achieved in open territory rather than in mature ecosystems where established competitors are struggling for a share of an existing market. By endlessly innovating, we grow through creating new frontiers rather than by undercutting our competitors.

Crucially, innovation is also fun and motivating, and keeps me feeling young, even at the ripe age of 72.

Beauty is what you learned from your childhood in nature. It is a hallmark of the elegance in the universe. All structures in nature have been distilled, purified, and stripped away until there is just enough. Just enough structure, just enough surface area, just enough colour – too much, and a more elegant and pared-down competitor will push you out; too little and you will not survive the fitness test when push comes to shove. Beauty is our refined eye for that which is just right in the world around us. And so beauty is at once one of the three pillars, and also a synthesis of the other two. When we have gotten the structure and space just right, and when we use our most recently advanced technical innovations to their maximum, we all see beauty. And it is that thread of beauty that has motivated your work for 35 years, and continues even in 2050. Good efforts so far, and all my best to those of you in 2015. There is a bright future ahead of you.

DaeWha

PS. And finally, your grandchild is here, and is enjoying reading all of those letters that you have written over the past 35 years.[2] Thinking about the next generation is now second nature, and today nobody finds you eccentric for writing letters to a child that would not be born for decades. ⌂

Institute for Computational Design (Professor Achim Menges) and the Institute of Building Structures and Structural Design (Professor Jan Knippers), ICD/ITKE Research Pavilion, University of Stuttgart, Germany, 2014

In the innovative work of this research group, robots weave structural elements from fibres in only the places where they are needed for performance.

Notes
1. When I was Design Director at Zaha Hadid Architects for the King Abdullah Petroleum Studies and Research Center (KAPSARC) project.
2. Letters to a grandchild have been one way of focusing my mind on the long-term relevance of my work. They can be found at www.daewhakang.com/letters.

Charles Jencks has form. One of the most influential architectural authors and thinkers of our time, he has been forecasting futures and anticipating trends for half a century. His 1971 book *Architecture 2000: Predictions and Methods* gazed into the crystal ball 29 years ahead of the millennium. Here he provides a comprehensive overview of the art of prediction and its widely divergent styles and approaches.

The art of prediction has divergent styles, from brainstorming to daydreaming, from forecasting to backcasting. This last genre was created by Edward Bellamy's *Looking Backward: 2000–1887*,[1] a successful rear-view polemic and American bestseller first published in 1888 that greatly influenced William Morris, Ebenezer Howard and much European architecture. Its counterpart today, Jonathon Porritt's *The World We Made* (2013),[2] rewinds the backcasting from 2050 to 2015, an optimistic look as if we had solved our ecological problems. Wishful thinking and its opposite twin, doom and gloom, bedevils prediction and makes people cast away such books. To succeed, the genre has to be subtle and complex, which Porritt is at times: he shows in some detail how we get to the green and pleasant land. Each step is a reaction to a particular catastrophe, to 'water riots in the Middle East of 2017', such things as nuclear terrorism and the great famines of the 2020s, and to climate change disasters of the 2040s. These push the world towards an effective global response and the New Jerusalem of 2050. It is a 'just-so' story, designed to end happily.

The Art of Prediction

Charles Jencks

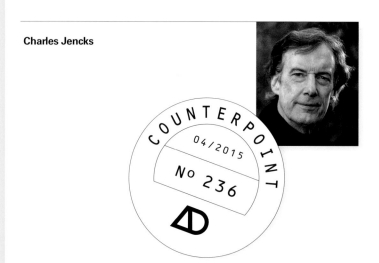

Scenarios and the SFW

Porritt's book shows that backcasting (like forecasting) must include the counter-scenarios and horrors. It cannot be called Futurology (reserve 'ology' for science) nor Futurism ('isms' describe art movements), but at best Futur*istics* (the suffix reserved for systematic study, as in statistics or heuristics). And for the study to succeed, what is needed at the start is a broad approach, the collection of many counter-trends that are underway, an eclectic approach covering the main political, social, cultural and economic forces driving the global world. One should not worry too much about whether a single trend will dominate, nor load the dice so that a favoured outcome always appears (and the reader turns off). Effective prediction is basically a sketch of large, inexorable forces, necessary to construct what in the 1960s was called the SFW – the Surprise-Free World. What the world would look like if all the dominating trends continued. This becomes the baseline; not something that will happen, but a shock of grim reality that one then varies with different scenarios.

Richard Buckminster Fuller was one important 'trender' of the 1960s who made the mistake of being too intelligent about technology and ecology, so he missed getting the baseline right (though he did highlight some inescapable forces). The SFW has to be constructed from big data coming from everywhere, and the master of this eclectic genre, who I was fortunate to meet in 1969, was Herman Kahn. He exploded with statistics on every branch of human endeavour, including figures on Arabs and hippies of whom he was not keen. You would imagine that, having swallowed the world, he would have a 'universal spirit' like Leonardo da Vinci, or Paul Valéry's Monsieur Teste, and be very fat; and he was all of this. An appetite for devouring knowledge, the Faustian mania, helps prediction as long as it is spread out in comprehensible streams of information. Its plausibility depends on this art of coherent evolution and revolution.

The danger is getting caught up in specialisation, and this happened from the 1970s after Futuristics declined. Just before then, many think tanks were at work in the US and Europe, from Kahn's Hudson Institute to the RAND Corporation, to Paris's Association Internationale Futuribles created by Bertrand de Jouvenel. The comparison of various futures or scenarios was the common goal of these generalist institutes that guided leaders during the Cold War. Today most prediction goes on in interest groups, those guiding corporations and stockbrokers, or is made by political assemblies such as Demos, or ideologues of a certain persuasion. Much is gained and lost with this historical shift in focus. Certainly the optimistic and generalist spirit, and especially its funding, has disappeared. But, with effective prediction, a robust SFW must be sketched first, and then from its architecture several opposite scenarios imagined – those that are good for the world, mediocre and bad. If one thing is certain about 2050, it will be the unsavoury mix of today plus a few more unexpected trends and a unique synthesis.

Poll the Experts and Think Sceptically

The second stage, that of specialist information, focuses on the particular breakthroughs imagined, and is called the Delphi technique (after the oracle that hedged her bets). At best it is a systematic poll of when, for instance, the architectural experts think that the smart toilet (or all the smart objects at home) will be owned by 50 per cent of the population, a time span of, say, 10 years from 2020 to 2030. At the 2014 Venice Architecture Biennale, Rem Koolhaas debated this inexorable trend of smart objects with the man who sold his company, Nest Labs, to Google for $3.2 billion. Tony Fadell was in on the invention of the iPod and iPhone, and the positive aspect of Rem's confrontation was the way he interviewed this expert, accepting the likely breakthroughs and distributions, but sceptically questioning how privacies would suffer when your toilet did not like your anti-green style of life (or whatever was politically correct at the moment).

The point of such critical thinking is that for every averaged trend, a resistant counter-trend is possible. For every Bush, Blair and Cameron escalating security fears, there might be a resistant Snowden. Prediction should be nuanced enough to get the dominating and counter-trends in the same chart (and in this issue of Δ, Molly Wright Steenson voices the alarm over smart objects that might survey us; Samsung has already produced one – see pp 110–13).

In fact, with both the varying SFW plus the Delphi technique, prediction can get a lot of global trends and breakthroughs somewhat right. The successful 1969 moon shot was an obvious prediction in 1965, given Kennedy's earlier promise and the Cold War; and there are some logical inevitabilities awaiting those who combine both methods.

A few personal comments. In writing *Architecture 2000: Predictions and Methods* in 1969 (it came out in 1971), I was inspired to construct varying scenarios by thinkers in different fields: by forecasters mentioned; by the Structuralist work of Claude Lévi-Strauss; by the art historian George Kubler and his wonderful speculation *The Shape of Time*; and of course by Darwin's evolutionary tree.[3] This clarified the idea of many species of architecture evolving simultaneously. The first chart I created was a structural diagram of polar opposites, a semantic space of possible architectures, those that cohered around three axes. What mattered was clustering the categories in as much opposition as possible; that is, filling the multi-dimensional space of *'futuribles'*, of possibles. Architects cluster together for historical and psychological reasons, and this means architectural traditions self-organise along coherent trajectories (even though they also jump between them, unlike biological species).

Knowing that history is partly circular (or repetitive like the revolutions of the planets) *and* linear (like technical evolution), I conceived the evolution in pulsating blobs, as species that oscillate in sync, and against each other. In effect, this was projecting the SFW forward, for the next 30 years, and plugging in many specific breakthroughs, predicted by the experts, where they might fit.

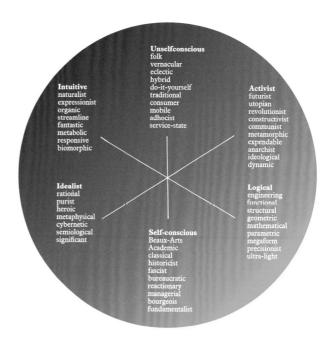

Charles Jencks

Traditions of architecture structural diagram

1920–2000

The six major traditions of architecture have a tendency to remain autonomous and stabilise around a common core.

Looking back 30 years later for the new millennium edition of the book (now called *Architecture 2000 and Beyond*),[4] I set out some positive and negative results. This can be seen by comparing the prediction with some movements that occurred. Positive predictions included the Biomorphic School, the Megaform movement, the '1984' reaction (the Fundamentalist and Prince Charles's Classical Revivalism), the Parametric movement, High Tech and Semiological architecture. Ill-conceived forecasts, such as the Revolutionist and Space Colonial movements, never turned into reality. Typically of predictors, when it went wrong I was guilty of following fashion, exotic ideas and technical possibilities like the cyborg and hydroponic architecture, not things that would affect society, nor the profession, nor even the avant-garde. At all events, the evolutionary chart was, structurally speaking, not a bad predictor itself.

The Importance of Combining Logical Inventions and Social Desire

One educated guess was inspired by a French prediction, Albert Robida's amazing logical ad hoc assembly of three existing technologies to produce the *téléphonoscope* (the telephone, record player and moving slide projector-scope of the 1880s). Robida's analytical invention led 70 years later to the ubiquitous home movie and television, and it underscores a main point: that to predict significant developments you have to combine social desire, the engine of the Surprise-Free World, with the inherent technical breakthroughs. Following this method, my ad hoc combination of 1969 predicted Google shopping of 30 years later. Motivated as democratic consumption in the 1960s, it shifted the balance of power away from the producer towards the user or consumer.[5] It combined

> To predict significant developments you have to combine social desire, the engine of the Surprise-Free World, with the inherent technical breakthroughs.

Charles Jencks

Evolutionary Tree showing architectural traditions pulsating like species

1969–2000

The 1969 predictions (left) versus some actualities (right). The 'Biomorphic' school occurred when Jencks predicted it (based on the forecast for biology being a leading science in the 1990s). 'Parametric' architecture took off later, in the 1990s, but not 'Space Colonial' (except for Norman Foster working for Richard Branson). In this very broad sense, roughly 50 per cent of the predictions in Jencks's book of 1969 were actualised.

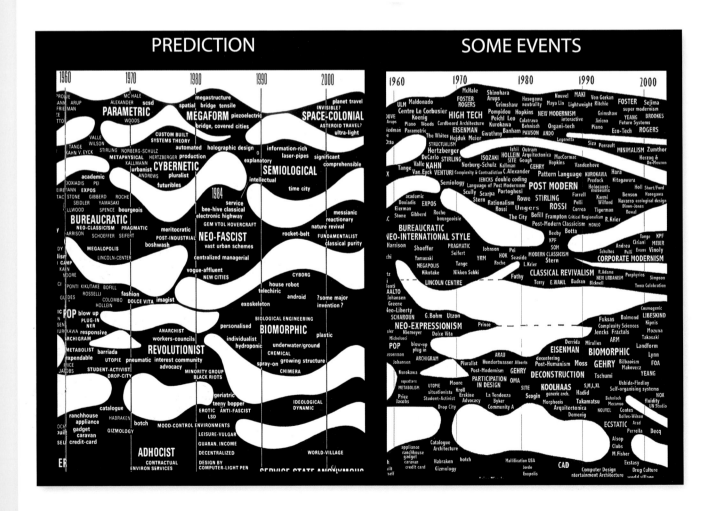

the growing computer power, shown left in the diagram, with the growing defence industry (the Pentagon, CIA, FBI, etc) (centre) and the home designer or architect (right), who sat at the TV monitor, scratching away with a light pen calling up the world's products, not unlike designers in a big architectural office today, except for the microfiche. Inevitably this diagram was inspired by the loathing for Big Brother and state terrorism – call it the Snowden resistance that is always around – plus such things as *The Whole Earth Catalog*. Little did I know that the US Defence Department was actually working on a related system, which led to the Internet, and more positively to the idea of the World Wide Web, in 1989. Like the *téléphonoscope,* my combination shows that logical ad hoc assemblies married to social desire can be spot on.

Albert Robida

Téléphonoscope from *Le Vingtième Siècle*

1883

A happy fat cat, Monsieur Ponto, sits back and watches *Faust* for the twelfth time, using this ad hoc combination of existing technologies (it predicted the home movie and TV).

Le Théâtre chez soi par le Telephonoscope.

Charles Jencks

Consumer democracy

1969

Google shopping and design predicted 30 years before the fact by assembling the existing technology and desiring more power in the hands of the user.

In 1999, when looking at the next 50 years for *Architecture 2000 and Beyond,* I made a series of Delphi predictions, but located them at specific dates rather than following the correct method of giving a range of times plus a median date. The reason was the lack of room to show this time span, and the fact that I did not have the resources to consult the experts.[6] Instead authoritative (and questionable) sources were consulted, but the average correct predictions remain somewhere at the 50 per cent level. For instance, in 2001 I forecast that 'The richest fifth of the world already owns 80% of the planet's wealth' (top) and that in 2005 (lower table) 'The rich double their income' – both good and easy predictions. But I missed the all-important crash of 2007/8, because I did not then understand such packaged debt vehicles that George Soros and Warren Buffet were lamenting (they did predict the world mess five years ahead). And I missed the much further widening of incomes ever since. The crash quadrupled the wealth disparity, as the superrich were bailed out. Cynics quipped it was socialism for the rich and capitalism for the poor, and the misery now can be predicted to affect more than the Greeks and Europe.

Note some other anomalies, for instance, discoveries in science. I see the 'origin of the universe' was meant to be found in 2012 – whereas the Planck Mission of April 2013 really determined its best date (13.82 billion years ago) – and the 'Dark matter riddle' was supposed to be unravelled (well, not yet, the darkness is only a little brighter). The hedged nature of such detailed forecasts typifies the genre: necessarily so because prediction is an art.

Arthur C Clarke was one of the best clairvoyants, while Thomas J Watson, the Chairman of IBM, is supposed to have made one of the greatest mis-predictions in history. Because he was called the 'world's greatest salesman', sceptics often quoted a howler of 1943 – 'I think there is a world market for about five computers' – though no one can find the original quote. Being technically smart, and socially wrong, often leads to such mistakes. But there is an argument that success in the art consists not in getting things right, but in making people think. Bertrand de Jouvenel puts this case in his 1961 French edition of *Futuribles* – the reasoned conjecture about

Charles Jencks

Events, breakthroughs and cultural shifts

1999

Some 100 Delphic predictions Jencks made in 1999.

Plausible events that would change the World

2000	2010	2020	2030	2040	2050	Never

Politics
*The richest fifth of world already owns 80% of planet's wealth
*National governments lose further power to multinationals, NGOs, and transnational organisations
*Nato, Asian & Block alliances govern regions
*Christian worship falls to nominal levels in Europe & UK, vague spirituality replaces faith
*EURO extends from Ireland to Hungary
*Catholics reunite Christians, ordain married men & women
*Muslim Anthrax attack on Israel/American targets
*North (rich) South (poor) divide leads to new block alliance
*Limited nuclear exchange between India & Pakistan
*Massive migration from South to North, especially from Africa
*United Nations resuscitated and given military force
*China overtakes USA as largest GDP and creates federal state
*Bioweapon/nerve gas attack on major western city
*Limited nuclear exchange in Asia
* Muslim block starts Cold War with the West a minority
*Multicultural America, whites
* Korea unified peacefully
* 50 nations with nuclear capability

Economy/Ecology
* Global warming increases storm damage
*Fish stocks plummet, oceans privatised by WTO
*Ozone hole starts to shrink for the first time
Middle Eastern War over water/ ecological problem
*Global warming further melts polar caps flooding low cities, Netherlands, Bangladesh, English Fens & Florida etc.
*Medicine becomes the biggest global industry
*Major earthquake in Los Angeles/Tokyo/Pacific Rim
*Alps' glaciers melt causing large avalanches
*Preventative medicine & positive health becomes key to economic growth
*One third of world immiserated in mega-ghettoes
*Pollution penalties introduced globally
*Dow at 50,000
*Ecological instabilities caused by runaway "Greenhouse"
*Super volcano erupts in Yellowstone National Park creating world freeze and famine

Social
*The rich double 2000 income
*Three major car companies merge and produce small, cheap and pollution-free hydrogen-fuelled car
*Single-parent family becomes norm in "First World"
*Global warming shifts Gulf Stream - Europe's climate becomes like Siberia
*China's ecological and medical problems immiserate half of population
*The rich quadruple 2000 income
*Private armies subcontracting by UN, USA & Japan
*3 Trading blocks. Europe, America & Asia restructure global trade for ecological imperatives
*Rising sea levels create 150 million environmental refugees
*Multinationals merge & hire private armies
*Security/terrorism the major social problem
*Global government -UNG- creates alienation in old USA
*Population 9 billion, slows because of economic improvements

This eclectic list of prediction, compiled from both authorative and questionable sources, provides hints for some general patterns. These became a catalyst for defining the evolutionary scenario in the new text at the end.

possible futures, a speculation within constrained limits of perhaps 5 to 30 years.[7] Opposite scenarios are dramatised to heighten choice, swing opinion, generate inventions – in short to change the history that will happen, to make mainstream prediction, the SFW, wrong.

Karl Marx and his polemical manifestoes did just that, as did Nietzsche and Le Corbusier, who also sought to change the future. Edward Bellamy in his *Looking Backward*[8] predicted successfully, like a very good novelist, but it is chastening to reflect that these last-mentioned soothsayers got as much badly wrong as right. I respect and admire Jonathon Porritt and his backcast from 2050, the best such narrative of its type. But the problem, again, is the limited focus on sustainability, for which he has been struggling as Chair of the Green Party and many other forums for the future. Values are brought into being by creation and argument, by persuasion and coercion, by luck and social movements and not by the reasoned calculus of some supreme being. Since I am a signed-up 'value pluralist' in the Isaiah Berlin tradition, it is easy to admit the value of Porritt's advocacy while asking for a more varied cultural picture of why the future might be very desirable.

TR Hamzah & Yeang

Menara Mesiniaga

Subang Jaya

Selangor, Malaysia

1992

The bioclimatic skyscraper with its spiral skycourts influenced many future green projects.

In effect, dogmatic architects advocate singular values rather well. They both predict the future they want, and persuade us to follow the inexorable trends they select. Le Corbusier, in the 1920s, repeated a forecast about mass-production houses in his polemic *Towards a New Architecture*: 'Industry, overwhelming us like a flood which rolls on towards its destined ends, has furnished us with new tools adapted to this new epoch, animated by the new spirit,'[9] and then he designed stunning images of 'machines-for-living'. Ken Yeang and Norman Foster, in the 1990s, echoed predictions of eco-doom and then designed in very different styles buildings that spiral upwards with many seductive green aspects. Leon Krier and Rem Koolhaas, with opposite values, cite tendencies that support their classical versus hybrid creations. Daniel Libeskind, as much as Frank Lloyd Wright 100 years earlier, is a prophet aiming to convince through all the rhetorical aids available to religious leaders in the past. Walter Gropius never tired of prophecy, nor do most creative architects, even when they run out of visions for the future. And thus prediction and advocacy necessarily get all mixed up together in architecture. This has happened since the time of Vitruvius, who advocated a futurism based on the past Greek architecture.

Architects, like doctors and politicians, are a future-oriented profession because by definition they all build on promises for the future. But they are trained in *selective* forecasting, rather than systematic thinking across professions. Hence the art of prediction carries two quite different kinds of valuable forecasts: those one-sided projections that persuade us through strength of vision; and those balanced and widely eclectic forecasts that persuade through logic and plausibility. We do not have to choose between them because neither tradition is about to stop. And in opposite ways both increase the value pluralism on offer. But it is worth emphasising that they are quite different kinds of competitive art, each taking skill and knowledge. ᗄ

Notes
1. Edward Bellamy, *Looking Backward: 2000–1887,* 1888: https://librivox.org/looking-backward-2000-1887-by-edward-bellamy/.
2. Jonathon Porritt, *The World We Made: Alex McKay's Story from 2050,* Phaidon (London), 2013
3. My first book of forecasts and its structural diagrams, *Architecture 2000: Predictions and Methods,* Studio Vista (London) and Praeger (New York), 1971, was influenced by the following: Claude Lévi-Strauss, *Structural Anthropology,* Doubleday Anchor Books (New York), 1963; George Kubler, *The Shape of Time,* Yale University Press (New Haven, CT), 1962; Herman Kahn with Anthony Wiener, *The Year 2000: A Framework for Speculation on the Next Thirty-Three Years,* MacMillan (New York), 1967; Bertrand de Jouvenel, *The Art of Conjecture,* Basic Books (New York), 1967.
4. Charles Jencks, *Architecture 2000 and Beyond,* John Wiley & Sons (Chichester), 2000, pp 4–5, 46–7.
5. Charles Jencks and Nathan Silver, *Adhocism: The Case for Improvisation,* Secker & Warburg (London), 1971, p 63; republished with a new introduction by MIT Press (Cambridge, MA), 2013.
6. Jencks, *Architecture 2000 and Beyond, op cit*; see the inside covers for these Delphi predictions.
7. Bertrand de Jouvenel, *Futuribles,* from his lecture transcript, RAND Interdepartmental Seminar, 30 November 1964: see www.rand.org/content/dam/rand/pubs/papers/2008/P3045.pdf.
8. Edward Bellamy, *op cit.*
9. See Le Corbusier, *Towards a New Architecture,* trans Frederick Etchells, The Architectural Press (London), 1927, p 12.

Paola Antonelli is the Senior Curator of Architecture and Design and Director of Research and Development at the Museum of Modern Art (MoMA) in New York. Her work investigates the influence of design on everyday experience, often including overlooked objects and practices, and combining design, architecture, art, science and technology. She lectures frequently at high-level global conferences and coordinates cultural discussions at the World Economic Forum in Davos. A true interdisciplinary, energetic and generous cultural thinker, she was recently rated as one of the top 100 most powerful people in the world of art by *Art Review*.

Janine Benyus is a biologist and author of six books, including *Biomimicry: Innovation Inspired by Nature* (William Morrow, 2002). She co-founded Biomimicry 3.8, an innovation consultancy bringing 3.8 billion years of brilliant ideas to the design table. Clients include BNIM, Boeing, General Electric, Gensler, Google, HOK, IDEO, Jacobs Engineering, Jaguar, Kohler, Levi's and Nike. She has been a keynote speaker at the American Institute of Architects (AIA), GreenBuild, International Interior Design Association (IIDA), Industrial Designers Society of America (IDSA), TED, and TED Global. Awards include the Cooper-Hewitt National Design Mind and Time's Heroes of the Environment.

Roberta L Bondar, the world's first neurologist in space, conducted international experiments on space mission STS 42. Subsequently, her international research team worked with NASA on neurological symptoms seen after space flight and connections to neurological diseases on earth. She is a professional nature and landscape photographer, and the author of four photo-essay books. Her fine art photographic works are found in private, corporate and institutional collections in Canada, the US and UK.

Alfredo Brillembourg trained at Columbia University and the Central University of Venezuela. He founded the interdisciplinary design practice Urban-Think Tank with Hubert Klumpner in Caracas in 1998. Since 2007, he and Klumpner have been guest professors at Columbia University, where they founded the Sustainable Living Urban Model Laboratory (SLUM Lab), and have held a Chair of Architecture and Urban Design at the ETH in Zurich since 2010. In his capacity as co-director of Urban-Think Tank, Brillembourg has been awarded the 2010 Ralph Erskine Award, the 2011 Holcim Gold Award for Latin America, and the 2012 Holcim Global Silver Award for innovative contributions to social and ecological design. He was also part of the Golden Lion-winning team at the 13th Venice Biennale for the Torre David/Gran Horizonte installation. In 2014, Brillembourg and Klumpner were selected, along with Aaron Betsky and Doreen Heng Liu, as the chief curators of the forthcoming Shenzhen/Hong Kong Bi-City Biennale of Urbanism/Architecture.

Tim Brown is CEO and President of IDEO, a global design and innovation firm. He participates in the World Economic Forum in Davos, Switzerland, and chairs the World Economic Forum Global Agenda Council on the Creative Economy. An industrial designer by training, he has given two TED Talks on the subjects of design and innovation: 'Serious Play' and 'Change by Design'. His book *Change By Design: How Design Thinking Transforms Organizations and Inspires Innovation* was published by HarperBusiness in 2009.

Thomas Fisher is a Professor at the School of Architecture and Dean of the College of Design at the University of Minnesota, having previously served as the Editorial Director of *Progressive Architecture* magazine. With degrees from Cornell and Case Western Reserve universities, he was recognised in 2005 as the fifth most published architecture writer in the US, with eight books, over 50 book chapters or introductions, and more than 325 articles.

Francesca Galeazzi is an architectural engineer with over 15 years' experience in sustainable development, and currently leads the sustainability team of Arup Associates in Shanghai. She has expertise in environmental sustainability strategies at both the urban and building scales, zero-carbon projects, climate change adaptation and mitigation, urbanisation and social sustainability. She is a regular speaker at international conferences and forums on sustainable architecture, and lectures at major universities in Europe and China.

Lisa Gansky is the author of bestseller *The Mesh: Why the Future of Business is Sharing* (Penguin, 2010), a primer on the Sharing Economy. She is Founder of Mesh Labs and the Instigator Collective. She is a serial entrepreneur, innovation adviser, angel investor, author and international speaker on the topics of social innovation, value creation and entrepreneurship. She is pathologically curious about shareable business models, rethinking value, waste and resilient design, renewable energy, urban innovation and the growing global rise of entrepreneurship.

Nataly Gattegno and Jason Kelly Johnson are the founding principals of Future Cities Lab, an experimental design studio, workshop and architectural think tank based in San Francisco. Since 2002 they have collaborated on a range of award-winning projects exploring the intersections of art and design with advanced fabrication technologies, robotics, responsive building systems and public space. Nataly and Jason are Associate Professors at the California College of the Arts.

Dan Hill is an Executive Director and Chief Design Officer at the Future Cities Catapult, a UK government-backed urban innovation agency. A designer and urbanist, he has previously held leadership positions at Fabrica, Sitra (the Finnish Innovation Fund), Arup, Monocle and the BBC. He has worked on major urban projects worldwide, from Barangaroo in Sydney to Low2No in Helsinki, Masdar in Abu Dhabi to the Northern Quarter in Manchester. He is an adjunct professor in the Design, Architecture and Building faculty at the University of Technology, Sydney, and in the School of Media and Communications at RMIT University in Melbourne.

Charles Jencks divides his time between lecturing, writing and designing in the US, UK and Europe. He is the author of *The Architecture of Hope: Maggie's Cancer Caring Centres* (Frances Lincoln, 2015), *The Story of Post-Modernism: Five Decades of Ironic, Iconic and Critical Architecture* (Wiley, 2011); *The Universe in the Landscape* (Frances Lincoln, 2011); and bestseller *The Language of Post-Modern Architecture* (re-issued as *The New Paradigm in Architecture* by Yale University Press, 2002). He has also written numerous other books on contemporary arts and building. His celebrated garden in Scotland is the subject of his book *The Garden of Cosmic Speculation* (Frances Lincoln, 2003), and in 2004 the Scottish National Gallery of Modern Art, Edinburgh, won the Gulbenkian Prize for Museums for his design, Landform Ueda. Landform projects have also been completed in Europe, and his current concern is working with Cern on an iconographic and green project. His ad hoc sculpture *Metaphysical Landscapes* was exhibited at Jupiter Artland outside Edinburgh in 2011. He has recently designed *The Crawick Multiverse,* which opened in Kirkconnel, Scotland, in June 2015.

AD ARCHITECTURAL DESIGN

2050

CONTRIBUTORS

Mitchell Joachim is a co-founder of Terreform ONE and an Associate Professor at New York University. He was formerly an architect at Gehry Partners and Pei Cobb Freed. He is a TED Senior Fellow and has been awarded fellowships with Moshe Safdie and the Martin Society for Sustainability at MIT. He was chosen by *Wired* magazine for 'The Smart List: 15 People the Next President Should Listen To'. He has won many awards including the Time Magazine Best Invention with the MIT Smart Cities Car. He is co-author of the books *Super Cells: Building with Biology* (TED Conferences, 2014) and *Global Design: Elsewhere Envisioned* (Prestel, 2014). His work has been exhibited at the Museum of Modern Art (MoMA) in New York and the Venice Biennale. He earned his PhD at MIT, MAUD at Harvard University and MArch at Columbia University.

Alexis Kalagas is a writer and researcher at Urban-Think Tank at ETH Zurich. Raised in Australia, he completed graduate studies in Geneva and Boston, where his research centred on the spatial dimensions of urban violence, and he holds bachelor degrees in political science and law from the University of Melbourne. He has previous experience as a foreign policy adviser in the Australian government focusing on Africa and the Middle East, and as the editor of a Geneva-based global media start-up, he is the guest-editor of the most recent issue of *SLUM Lab* magazine and recently completed a book with Alfredo Brillembourg and Hubert Klumpner exploring a post-crisis vision for the city of Athens.

DaeWha Kang is a designer and architect in London. During his time with Zaha Hadid Architects he was the design director of the KAPSARC energy research centre in Saudi Arabia, the office's first LEED-Platinum certified building. He established DaeWha Kang Design in 2014 to combine his deep passion for beauty and innovation in design with an agenda of measurably improving human wellbeing through architecture.

Hubert Klumpner trained at Columbia University and the University of Applied Arts Vienna. He founded the interdisciplinary design practice Urban-Think Tank with Alfredo Brillembourg in Caracas in 1998. He is Dean of the Department of Architecture at the Chair of Architecture and Urban Design at the ETH Zurich.

Karin Lepasoon was most recently Executive Vice President and member of the Senior Executive Team at Skanska, a leading international project development and construction company headquartered in Stockholm. She held global responsibility for strategy, communications, investor relations, sustainability, IT and knowledge management. In 2015 she joined the Stockholm-based private equity firm Nordic Capital as Director of Communications, ESG (environment, social and governance standards) and HR. She holds a Master of Laws from the University of Lund in Sweden and a Master of European Community Laws from the University of Leiden in the Netherlands.

Tim Maughan is a British writer currently based in Brooklyn, who uses both fiction and non-fiction to explore issues around cities, art, class and technology. His debut short story collection *Paintwork* received critical acclaim when released in 2011, and his story 'Limited Edition' was shortlisted for the 2012 British Science Fiction Association (BSFA) short fiction award. His non-fiction work regularly appears in a number of publications including *New Scientist, Arc* and *Icon,* and he has recently given talks at Princeton School of Architecture, HASTAC 2014 in Lima, Lambeth Council in London, and Sonic Acts in Amsterdam. He sometimes makes films as well.

Alex McDowell is the Creative Director of 5D GlobalStudio, Professor of Practice at the University of Southern California (USC) School of Cinematic Arts, Media Arts + Practice, and the William Cameron Menzies Endowed Chair in Production Design Director at the USC World Building Media Lab, USC World Building Institute. His production design on *Minority Report* (Steven Spielberg, 2002) solidified his world-building method and interest in reimagining storytelling. His many credits include *Fight Club* (David Fincher, 1999) and *Charlie and the Chocolate Factory* (Tim Burton, 2005). He currently applies world building across industries at 5D GlobalStudio, which combines emergent technologies with interactive narratives for clients (Nike, Boeing and Intel, among others). His research lab at USC investigates the future of narrative, cities and technology.

Philip Nobel is the Editorial Director of SHoP Architects and the author of *Sixteen Acres: Architecture and the Outrageous Struggle for the Future of Ground Zero* (Metropolitan Books, 2005). His writing has appeared in *Artforum,* the *New York Times, Metropolis,* the *London Review of Books* and elsewhere.

Franz Oswald is an architect, Professor at ETH Zurich, and Head of AUS – Office for Architecture and Urban Studies in Bern, an architecture and urban design practice and consulting agency. He is the former dean of architecture at ETH Zurich, and director of its ORLInstitute, President of SCUPAD in Salzburg, and an international juror and expert on university reform in Ethiopia. He is the former programme leader of the Future Cities Laboratory at ETH Singapore, and a co-initiator of the Amhara Model Town Buranest and founding president of the Nestown Group. His many projects and publications focus on theory, education, urban design and planning.

Emily Pilloton is the founder of the non-profit design agency Project H. She has written books, shared ideas on stages around the world, and debated with Stephen Colbert on the importance of humanitarian design. An architect by training, she can most often be found welding with her 10-year-old Camp H girls or co-teaching her design/build high school programme Studio H in Berkeley, California.

Enric Sala is a National Geographic Explorer-in-Residence dedicated to help protect the last wild places in the ocean. His Pristine Seas project was key in inspiring the protection of over 2.2 million square kilometres of ocean in Chile, Gabon, Kiribati, Costa Rica, the Pitcairn Islands and US Pacific waters. He has received many awards, including the 2008 Young Global Leader at the World Economic Forum, and 2013 Lowell Thomas Award of the Explorers Club.

Mark Watts serves as the Executive Director of the C40 Cities Climate Leadership Group. Prior to joining C40, he was, from 2008, the Director of Arup's energy consulting team. Focused on cities and sustainability, he led Arup's partnership with C40. Before joining Arup, he was the climate change and sustainable transport adviser to the Mayor of London where he led the development of London's Climate Change Action Plan.

Molly Wright Steenson is an assistant professor in the School of Journalism and Mass Communication at the University of Wisconsin-Madison. She researches the history of interactivity, architecture and computation and holds a PhD in Architecture from Princeton University.

Liam Young is an architect who operates in the spaces between design, fiction and futures. He is founder of the think tank Tomorrow's Thoughts Today, a group whose work explores the possibilities of fantastic, speculative and imaginary urbanisms. He also runs a graduate studio at Princeton University and is a co-founder of the Unknown Fields Division, a nomadic studio based at the Architectural Association (AA) in London that travels on annual expeditions to the ends of the earth to investigate extreme landscapes, alien terrains and industrial ecologies. His projects develop fictional speculations as critical instruments to survey the consequences of emerging environmental and technological futures.

What is Architectural Design?

Founded in 1930, *Architectural Design* (△) is an influential and prestigious publication. It combines the currency and topicality of a newsstand journal with the rigour and production qualities of a book. With an almost unrivalled reputation worldwide, it is consistently at the forefront of cultural thought and design.

Each title of △ is edited by an invited Guest-Editor, who is an international expert in the field. Renowned for being at the leading edge of design and new technologies, △ also covers themes as diverse as architectural history, the environment, interior design, landscape architecture and urban design.

Provocative and inspirational, △ inspires theoretical, creative and technological advances. It questions the outcome of technical innovations as well as the far-reaching social, cultural and environmental challenges that present themselves today.

For further information on △, subscriptions and purchasing single issues see:

www.architectural-design-magazine.com

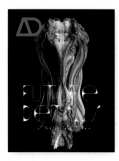

Volume 84 No 4
ISBN 978 1118 522530

Volume 84 No 5
ISBN 978 1118 613481

Volume 84 No 6
ISBN 978 1118 663301

Volume 85 No 1
ISBN 978 1118 759066

Volume 85 No 2
ISBN 978 1118 700570

Volume 85 No 3
ISBN 978 1118 829011